Instructor's Manual

to accompany

Handbook for Critical Reading

Don Meagher

Miami–Dade Community College

Fort Worth Philadelphia San Diego New York Orlando Austin San Antonio
Toronto Montreal London Sydney Tokyo

Contents

Harcourt Brace & Company

1

Teaching with

Handbook for Critical Reading

Handbook for Critical Reading focuses primarily on the reading of nonfiction, with argumentative and persuasive writing as the core, but with substantial references to college textbooks, fiction, and poetry. The word "critical" in the title suggests a focus on skills and strategies that are essential for comprehension in general and that deal with the analysis and evaluation of persuasive writing in particular.

What makes this book different from most other reading texts is the absence of practice exercises that accompany passages. This allows for versatility, making it possible for an instructor to use the book to accompany any choice of readings. This instructor's manual contains duplicable exercises that go with each chapter and that can be used either as exercises or as quizzes.

Most sections of each chapter begin with an explanation of a reading skill or strategy, then follow with an illustrative passage, and end with an analysis of the passage in terms of the topic under discussion.

A Rationale for *Handbook for Critical Reading*

Because there are so many excellent reading texts available now that combine reading selections, questions, and skills instruction, including many with current and relevant readings, *Handbook for Critical Reading* has been designed to provide explanations of key reading skills and strategies that can be used to accompany an anthology or other collection of readings that lack such direct instruction. As such, this book should fill a gap for reading teachers who prefer using an anthology, news magazines, newspapers, or other readings to the skill-based structure of many reading texts, but who also want to provide students with some general explanations of reading strategies.

My interest in writing this book has been kindled both by my reading in the literature of reading and composition theory and by my experience teaching reading to community college students. My years of teaching college reading have led me to want to write the kind of textbook, such as this, that I have never been able to find—a clear, concise, and thorough introduction for students on how to evaluate texts for what is necessary to understand and remember for practical purposes and for what is also worth adding to their understanding of the world.

Harcourt Brace & Company

Suggested Use of *Handbook for Critical Reading* in a College Course

Handbook for Critical Reading is designed to be used to supplement another source of readings, with or without exercises, that lacks detailed explanations of skills and strategies. The book is designed mainly for students in introductory college reading courses, but because of the focus on general strategies involved in critical reading, it could also be used in more advanced classes, in English composition courses, or in academic support labs.

The chapters focus on reading skills and strategies, including study strategies, comprehension, interpretation, analysis, and evaluation. Each chapter contains sample explanations and examples. The explanations are in language that a first-year college student should be able to understand and do not include academic or pedagogical jargon. The examples are included to guide students through the types of analysis that the text explains.

The book can be conveniently used over a ten-week period during a semester by assigning one chapter each week, along with whatever readings would be appropriate. The appropriate **Chapter Review** handouts, duplicated from this instructor's manual, can also be used with a chapter either as an assignment to complete while students read the chapter or afterwards as a quiz. Or if an instructor desires, some of the chapters lend themselves to division in order to spread assignments out over more weeks during a term.

In addition, this instructor's manual contains duplicable **Generic Exercise/quizzes** and **Exercise/Quizzes for Specific Readings**, both of which correspond to each of the ten chapters in *Handbook for Critical Reading*. The **generic exercise/quizzes** are meant to be used with whatever readings an instructor wants to assign to go along with the chapters. The reading selections that the **Exercise/Quizzes for Specific Readings** refer to are all contained in *An Introduction to Critical Reading* compiled by Thomas Barnwell and Leah McCraney.

In addition to being used as quizzes or exercises, any of these duplicable handouts could be used as part of a portfolio assignment. The following is a list of some anthologies, textbooks, other collections of readings, and news magazines that *Handbook for Critical Reading* could accompany quite effectively:

News Magazines

Time Magazine

Newsweek

U.S. News & World Report

Anthologies Intended for College Reading Courses

Barnwell, Thomas, and Leah McCraney, Eds. (1997). *An Introduction to Critical Reading*, Third Edition. Fort Worth: Harcourt Brace College Publishers.

Johnson, Harriet, Ed. (1986). *Ideas in Context: Strategies for College Reading*. Belmont, CA: Wadsworth.

Fjeldstad , Mary C., Ed. (1994). *The Thoughtful Reader: A Whole Language Approach to College Reading*. Fort Worth: Harcourt Brace College Publishers.

Grinols, Anne Bradstreet, Ed. (1988). *Critical Thinking: Reading and Writing across the Curriculum*. Belmont, CA: Wadsworth.

Jacobus, Lee, Ed. (1993). *Improving College Reading*, Sixth Edition. Fort Worth: Harcourt Brace College Publishers.

Milan, Dianne, Ed. (1992). *Improving Reading Skills*, Second Edition. New York: McGraw Hill.

Pacheco, Beth M., Ed. (1992). *Academic Reading and Study Skills: A Theme-Centered Approach*. Fort Worth: Harcourt Brace College Publishers.

Pokras , Judith, Ed. (1996). *Contexts in the College Curriculum*. Belmont, CA: Wadsworth.

Sayers, Kari, Ed. (1996). *Views and Visions: Diverse Readings on Universal Themes*. Belmont, CA: Wadsworth.

Short Anthologies Intended for Composition Courses

Aaron, Jane E., Ed. (1993). *The Compact Reader: Short Essays by Theme and Form*. Boston: Bedford Books of St. Martin's Press.

Ackley, Katherine Anne, Ed. (1992). *Essays from Contemporary Culture*. Fort Worth: Harcourt Brace College Publishers.

Atwan, Robert, Ed. (1992). *Ten on Ten: Major Essayists on Recurring Themes*. Boston: Bedford Books of St. Martin's Press.

Hayes, Christopher G., and Patricia J. McAlexander, Eds. (1995). *The Townsend Thematic Reader*. Marlton, NJ: Townsend Press.

King, Anne Mills, Ed. (1993). *The Engaging Reader*, Second Edition. New York: Macmillan.

Seyler, Dorthy U., Ed. (1992). *Patterns of Reflection: A Reader*. New York: Macmillan.

Smart, William, Ed. (1995). *Eight Modern Essayists*, Sixth Edition. New York: St. Martin's Press.

Warner, J. Sterling, Judith Hilliard, and Vincent Piro, Eds. (1995). *Visions across the Americas: Short Essays for Composition*, Second Edition. Fort Worth: Harcourt Brace College Publishers.

Valeri-Gold, Maria, and Mary P. Deming, Eds. (1994). *Making Connections through Reading and Writing*. Belmont, CA: Wadsworth.

Young, Diana, Ed. (1994). *Cartographies: Contemporary American Essays*. Boston: Bedford Books of St. Martin's Press.

Longer Anthologies Intended for Composition Courses

Clegg, Cynthia Susan, Ed. (1988). *Critical Reading and Writing Across the Disciplines*. New York: Holt, Rinehart and Winston.

Colombo, Gary, Robert Cullen, and Bonnie Lisle, Eds. (1992). *Rereading America: Cultural Contexts for Critical Thinking and Writing*. Boston: Bedford Books of St. Martin's Press.

Eschholz, Paul, Alfred Rosa, and Virginia Clark. (1994). *Language Awareness*, Sixth Edition. New York: St. Martin's Press

Jacobus, Lee A., Ed. (1994). *A World of Ideas: Essential Readings for College Writers*, Fourth Edition. Boston: Bedford Books of St. Martin's Press.

Atwan, Robert, Ed. (1993). *Our Times 3: Reading from Recent Periodicals*. Boston: Bedford Books of St. Martin's Press.

2

Review Exercises/Quizzes

for

Handbook for Critical Reading

Following the answer key, you will find duplicable handouts that can be used with the appropriate chapters as exercises to complete while reading the chapter or as quizzes to be given afterwards. The title of each exercise/quiz is the same as for each chapter of *Handbook for Critical Reading*. The items in each exercise/quiz include questions regarding the contents of the chapter and items asking students to apply what they have learned.

Review Exercise/Quiz
Answer Key

Chapter 1 Review: Reading Textbooks

1.	organized	16.	D	29.	E
2.	B	17.	G	30.	D
3.	D	18.	A	31.	A
4.	A	19.	B		B
5.	A	20.	previewing,		C
6.	C		(active) reading,	32.	C
7.	B		reviewing	33.	C
8.	D	21.	B	34.	B
9.	A	22.	H	35.	4
10.	D	23.	A	36.	2
11.	C	24.	D	37.	3
12.	D	25.	F	38.	1
13.	F	26.	I	39.	D
14.	C	27.	G	40.	A
15.	E	28.	C		

Chapter 2 Review: Defining Words

1. C	14. tain	30. ence
2. synonym, antonym	15. the	31. ory
	16. bi	32. ism
3. A	17. poly	33. ist
4. D	18. semi	34. ship

5. C
   B
   A
	19. contra	35. ize

	20. mal	36. guide words
6. and	21. un	37. pronunciation
7. bio	22. circum	38. part of speech
8. chron	23. extra	39. word origin
9. dic	24. re	40. definitions
10. equi	25. ante	41. synonyms
11. grat	26. able	42. label
12. mort	27. ful	43. definitions
13. path	28. less	44. main entry
	29. ly	45. related form

Chapter 3 Review: Recognizing Main Ideas

1. topic
   main idea
   topic sentence
   supporting details
   thesis
	7. A
	8. D
	9. C
	10. B
	11. A
		C.: A
		C.2.: D
		C.3.b.: B

2. C	12. A	16. F
3. D	13. D	C

4. major
   minor
	14. B
	15. Thesis: F
		E
		   A

5. E	B.1.: C	D
6. B	B.3.: E	B

Chapter 4 Review: Identifying Organizational Patterns

1. transitions
   organizational patterns
2. D
3. I
4. L
5. K
6. E
7. J
8. F
9. G
10. H
11. A
12. C
13. B
14. and
    addition
15. affect (influence)
    cause and effect
16. within (inside)
    location
17. even though (although)
    contrast
18. therefore (consequently, as a
        result, hence)
    cause and effect
19. for example (for instance)
    example
20. indeed (in fact)
    emphasis
21. branch (field, school, aspect)
    classification
22. alike (similarly)
    comparison
23. until
    time order
24. also
    addition
25. in conclusion (in sum)
    summary
26. H
27. K
28. D
29. A
30. C
31. J
32. B
33. I
34. E
35. F
36. G
37. classification
38. cause and effect
39. analogy
40. spatial
41. clarification through example
42. cause and effect
43. chronological order
44. chronological order
45. chronological order
46. cause and effect
47. contrast
48. general
    specific
    specific
    general
    importance
49. A
50. A

Chapter 5 Review: Using Inference

1. inference
drawing conclusions
purpose
tone

2. inform
persuade
entertain

3. words
ideas (concepts,
    details, points)

4. B

5. A

6. D

7. D

8. C

9. B

10. A

11. D

12. persuade
respectful

13. inform
tragic

14. persuade
critical

15. inform

ironic

16. persuade
critical

17. entertain
sarcastic

18. persuade
.respectful

19. persuade
optimistic

20. inform
objective

Chapter 6 Review: Interpreting Figurative Language

1. denotation
connotation

2. D

3. A

4. H

5. B

6. G

7. C

8. E

9. F

10. positive

11. negative

12. negative

13. positive

14. D

15. A

16. C

17. A

18. simile

19. personification

20. metaphor

21. simile

22. hyperbole

23. metaphor

24. metaphor

25. idiom

26. symbolism
(refers to working
class)

27. symbolism
(refers to youth)

28. metaphor

29. simile

30. irony

Chapter 7 Review: Reading Literature

1. G	15. C	29. B
2. D	16. D	30. rhythm
3. K	17. B	31. rhyme
4. C	18. setting	32. free verse
5. F	19. characters	33. emotion
6. A	20. plot	34. imagery
7. E	21. point of view	35. significance
8. H	22. theme	36. effect
9. J	23. effect	37. B
10. B	24. D	38. C
11. I	25. A	39. D
12. F	26. B	40. C
13. A (or E)	27. D	
14. E (or A)	28. D	

Chapter 8 Review: Recognizing Persuasive Writing

1. fact	12. A	27. F
2. opinion	13. B	28. B
3. opinion	14. C	29. C
4. value words	15. C	30. A
opinion	16. B	31. C
5. weasel words	17. B	32. D
6. slanting	18. A	33. F
7. bias	19. C	34. E
8. opinion	20. D	35. B
good, great,	21. G	36. A
dangerous	22. C	37. A
9. fact/opinion	23. E	38. B
worst, waste	24. B	39. B
10. fact	25. H	40. C
11. fact	26. A	

Chapter 9 Review: Analyzing Arguments

1. argument
   thesis
   support
   assumptions
2. D
3. F
4. A
5. H
6. C
7. B
8. E
9. G
10. factual
11. value
12. factual
13. value
14. factual
15. value
16. value
17. F
18. A
19. H
20. E
21. B
22. C
23. G
24. D
25. I
26. factual
27. observation
28. expert opinion
29. facts
30. statistics
31. author's qualifications
32. expert opinion
33. value
34. appeal to values
35. appeal to values
36. C
37. A
38. D
39. B
40. B

Chapter 10 Review: Evaluating Arguments

1. C
2. A
3. D
4. A
5. D
6. B
7. B
8. A
9. B
10. A
11. B
12. C
13. A
14. A
15. D
16. A (or C)
17. B
18. A
19. B
20. C
21. D
22. C
23. A

Chapter 1 Review:

Reading Textbooks

1. Before you begin reading a textbook for the first time, it helps to know how it is ______ _________________________________ so you can use it most easily and get the most out of it.

______ 2. In the preface of a textbook, you will usually find

    A. a description of the complete contents of the book.
    B. enough to get a general idea of what to expect in the book.
    C. statements that suggest the author's bias or prejudice.
    D. definitions of important vocabulary words used in the book.

______ 3. The table of contents of a textbook can help you to see

    A. all of the ideas contained in the text.
    B. significant supplemental information.
    C. the author's purpose for writing the book.
    D. how the major ideas are related to one another.

______ 4. The appendices in a book contain

    A. additional information to supplement the main text.
    B. clear discussions of the implications of what the text has discussed.
    C. definitions of technical terms and other key words used in the text.
    D. an alphabetical listing of the main points discussed in the text.

______ 5. In the back of many textbooks, you will find a glossary that provides

    A. definitions of specialized words used in the book.
    B. interpretations of figurative expressions used in the book.
    C. explanations of ideas not otherwise explained in the text.
    D. discussions of key concepts to supplement the contents of the book.

______ 6. Using the index in a textbook can help you to

    A. identify the main topics contained in each chapter of the book.
    B. understand the author's purpose for organizing the book in the way it is.
    C. quickly and easily locate information contained in the book.
    D. define key words used in the text that are not defined elsewhere.

_______   7.   By reading introductory material that begins a textbook chapter, you can gain

   A.   a better understanding of what had been discussed in the previous chapter.
   B.   a framework of information, which will make it easier to understand and remember what you will read.
   C.   information of special interest that helps clarify some general ideas contained in the chapter.
   D.   a sense of the author's background that will help understand where he or she is coming from.

_______   8.   Sometimes a chapter begins with a list of key terms that can help you to

   A.   have a general understanding of the contents of the chapter.
   B.   develop an understanding of the author's level of sophistication.
   C.   review ideas presented in previous chapters so you can better understand what you will read.
   D.   know ahead of time the definitions of some of the important words that will appear in the chapter.

_______   9.   Marginal notes or questions provided in the text can be quite useful for

   A.   understanding the material as you read it and reviewing it afterwards.
   B.   copying for your own notes.
   C.   understanding key terms used in the chapter.
   D.   seeing how specific examples illustrate more general points.

_______ 10.   Inserts are often provided throughout a chapter that contain

   A.   statements of the author's opinion regarding the contents.
   B.   references to ideas discussed in other chapters.
   C.   lists of reference material that can be read for additional information.
   D.   information of some special interest meant to clarify more general ideas.

_______ 11.   You will often find review questions and a summary at the end of a chapter that are ideal for

   A.   assessing the value of the contents.
   B.   previewing the contents of the next chapter.
   C.   reinforcing what you have learned and studying for a test.
   D.   helping you decide what information to include in an outline.

_______ 12. To fully understand graphic illustrations in a textbook chapter, you should always read

A. the title.
B. any key or legend.
C. the caption.
D. All of the above.

INSTRUCTIONS: Next to each type of graphic illustration, write the letter from the description on the right that matches it.

13. _______ Map

14. _______ Diagram

15. _______ Flow Chart

16. _______ Pie Graph

17. _______ Line Graph

18. _______ Bar Graph

19. _______ Table

A. Represents amounts.

B. Lists facts or statistics in columns and rows.

C. Depicts an outline drawing of an object.

D. Shows percentages of a whole.

E. Represents a step-by-step procedure process.

F. Shows specific geographical areas.

G. Represents changes.

---

20. Textbook reading strategies, such as *SQ3R* and other methods, involve three basic stages:

_____________________, _____________________, and _____________________.

INSTRUCTIONS: Match the textbook reading strategies on the left with their definitions on the right by writing the letter of your choice in each space:

21. _______ Surveying

22. _______ Questioning

23. _______ Marking

24. _______ Annotating

25. _______ Notetaking

A. Highlight, underline, or circle the main points while you read.

B. Get an overview by skimming the main points.

C. Organize your annotations or notes to reinforce your learning.

D. Write notes in your own words in the margins.

26. _______   Reciting

27. _______   Reviewing

28. _______   Outlining and Mapping

29. _______   Paraphrasing and
             Summarizing

E.   Express the key points in your own
     words to test your understanding.

F.   Jot down notes in some organized
     way on paper.

G.   Read over what you have marked,
     annotated, and noted and question
     yourself concerning the main points.

H.   Identify the essential information by
     turning headings into questions.

I.   Repeat to yourself the essence of what
     you have just read or of your notes.

_______ 30. Outlining and mapping are similar to summarizing in that all three involve

   A.   listing the author's main points.
   B.   a graphic organization of the author's main points.
   C.   writing down the author's main points in a coherent narrative.
   D.   restating the author's main points.

_______ 31. Which of the following are factors to consider when deciding how fast you
            choose to read something?
            (Choose as many as you think are appropriate.)

   A.   Your purpose for reading.
   B.   The type of material you are reading.
   C.   The difficulty of the material you are reading.
   D.   Your own background as a reader.

_______ 32. Skimming is a useful strategy to help you

   A.   locate specific information.
   B.   understand the main points an author is making.
   C.   get a quick overview of the contents or of the author's perspective.
   D.   remember the author's main points and important supporting details.

_______ 33. Scanning is a useful strategy when you need to

   A.   understand the contents of an article.
   B.   recognize the author's main points.
   C.   look up a word in a dictionary.
   D.   study a chapter in a textbook.

_______ 34. When taking a reading test with passages, it is best to first

    A. pay careful attention to the details.
    B. read the passage quickly but carefully to understand its main ideas.
    C. read the questions carefully so you know what to look for in the passage.
    D. scan the passage for specific details that you think might be significant.

INSTRUCTIONS: When answering multiple-choice questions on an exam, there are strategies that can make the process easier. Arrange the following strategies in the order that it would be most effective to do them in by writing the numbers

1, 2, 3, or 4 in a space next to each one:

_______ 35. Find an answer that most closely matches the one you have come up with for yourself.

_______ 36. Try to come up with what you think the answer should be before looking at the answer choices.

_______ 37. Carefully consider each answer choice before making your final decision.

_______ 38. Make sure that you understand exactly what the question is asking.

_______ 39. An effective way to prepare for an essay exam is to first

    A. reread the chapters that the exam will cover.
    B. look over your notes and annotations.
    C. review the questions you had formulated in your previewing of the chapter.
    D. anticipate the types of questions that might be asked.

_______ 40. Once you are actually faced with an essay question on an exam, you want to be sure that you begin by

    A. understanding exactly what the question is asking.
    B. having your notes with you.
    C. mentally reviewing the main points you have studied.
    D. outlining what you plan to say.

Harcourt Brace & Company

Chapter 2 Review:

Defining Words

_______ 1. When you come across an unfamiliar word in your reading, the context often provides clues to help you figure out its meaning through

A. a dictionary definition.
B. any identifiable word parts in the word.
C. the surrounding words in a sentence or paragraph.
D. the main idea of the paragraph and the major supporting details.

2. An unfamiliar word may be defined or explained in the sentence or surrounding sentences, but sometimes you can figure out its meaning if a word of the same or similar meaning is used nearby; such a word is called a ___________________.
At other times, you may find a word of the opposite or contrasting meaning, which is called an ___________________.

_______ 3. One of the most common context clues is provided when an author gives an example that illustrates the meaning of a word. Which of the following is an *example* of a language?

A. Spanish
B. A human communication system based on vocal sounds
C. Linguistic
D. Verbal symbols

_______ 4. If no other context clue is present to suggest the meaning of an unfamiliar word, sometimes its meaning can be guessed from the

A. definition provided in a glossary.
B. margin notes.
C. illustrations accompanying the text.
D. surrounding details or mood.

5. The meaning of an unfamiliar word can often be figured out through word analysis, which involves understanding the word parts that make it up. Match the following word parts on the left with their definitions on the right:

Root _________   A. A word element or group of letters added at the end of
                                  a word to form a different part of speech.

Prefix _________

                             B. The most basic part of a word that gives it its basic meaning.

Suffix _________

                             C. A word element or group of letters added at the beginning of a word to form a new word.

INSTRUCTIONS: Complete each of the following sentences with a root, prefix, or suffix that makes sense considering the meaning of the sentence. You will find a word in each sentence that either means the same thing as the word part or that is related to it in some way that provides a hint:

Roots

6. If you can hear something, it is _______________ <u>ible</u>.

7. Something that is produced by a living organism, is said to be _________ <u>genic.</u>

8. A narrative tells a story by relating a _______ <u>ology</u> of events that occur over a time period.

9. A blessing that is conferred or said is a <u>bene</u> _________ <u>tion</u>.

10. Two things that are of equal distance from each other are said to be ______ <u>idistant.</u>

11. To feel thanks is to have _________ <u>itude.</u>

12. A funeral director is called a ________ <u>tician.</u>

13. To identify with or understand what another person is feeling is to <u>em</u> _______ <u>ize</u> with her.

14. An object designed to hold something is called a <u>con</u> _____________ <u>er.</u>

15. A belief in one god is called <u>mono</u> _________ <u>ism</u>.

Prefixes

16.   To divide or separate something into two parts is to _______________ furcate it.

17.   If something is decorated in many colors, it is said to be _________ chrome.

18.   A substance such as silicon that is better electrical conductor than insulation but not as good a conductor as some other substance is called a _______________ conductor.

19.   A difference between two things is called a ___________ st.

20   To fail or operate poorly is to ________ function.

21.   Someone who is not noticing something can be said to be _________ aware.

22.   When Ferdinand Magellan sailed around the globe, he is said to have ___________ navigated the earth.

23.   Maneuvers performed by an astronaut outside of his spacecraft are said to be __________ vehicular activity.

24.   To return to an earlier or less advanced stage is to _________ gress.

25.   The time before the American Civil War is known as the ________ bellum period.

Suffixes

26.   Something that can be easily moved is port_________.

27.   Someone who is full of optimism is very hope___________ about the future.

28.   A person who is without fault in a situation can be said to be blame___________.

29.   An animal that is very fast and agile is one that moves quick__________.

30.   An action that has taken place is an occur___________.

31.   A greenhouse or a place where plants are arranged for display is called a conservat____________.

32.   The religious belief held by most of the people of India is Hindu_________.

33.   A professional in the field of biology is called a biolog_________.

34.   The condition of having something in one's possession is called owner_________.

35.   To combine separate elements into a coherent whole is to synthes____________ them.

36. When you cannot figure out the meaning of a word on your own, you can of course
     use a dictionary. The easiest way to find a word when looking through a dictionary is
     to refer to the ______________________ at top of each page.

INSTRUCTIONS: Fill in the blanks around these sample dictionary entries. Choose
                from the following list to identify the different features pointed to in
                the entries. Notice that you will need to use one of them twice:

Main Entry

Pronunciation

Part of Speech

Definitions

Synonyms

Related Form

Label

Word Origin

37.   38.   39.

knowl•edge (nol´ij) n. [ME, fr. *knowelechen*, to
recognize] 1. The state or condition of knowing.
                                                       40.
2. Awareness, familiarity, or acquaintance gained
through study or experience. 3. The sum or body
of what has been learned, inferred, or perceived.   41. —
knowledgeable *adj.* *Syns*: information, lore, wisdom
                                          42.
known (nön) adj. generally recognized. —v. p.p. of
know.

knuck (nuk) n. *Informal.* Knuckle.
knuck•le (nuk´əl) n. [ME, fr. *knokel*] A joint or
area around a joint, esp. those joining a finger to
the hand. — *v.* , **-led, -ling.** To press or hit with
the knuckles. —*verb phrases,* **knuckle down.** To
seriously apply oneself. **Knuckle under.** To give
in to pressure.

45.

44.

43.

Chapter 3 Review:
Recognizing Main Ideas

1. A nonfiction reading passage is usually about a certain general subject or __________.

Each paragraph in the passage usually has a __________ __________ that represents

the point made about the subject in that paragraph. A sentence in the paragraph that

states this point is called a __________ __________.

The __________ __________ then explain or illustrate the central

point of the paragraph. In a selection composed of several paragraphs, the overall

point of the entire passage or essay is known as the __________.

______   2. To get a sense of the topic of a passage, ask yourself the question
     A. "What is the point?"
     B. "Why am I reading this?"
     C. "Who or what is it about?"
     D. "What is the author trying to accomplish?"

______   3. To figure out the complete main idea, ask yourself the question
     A. "Why should I care about this passage?"
     B. "Who or what is this passage about?"
     C. "Is the author representing information in an unbiased manner?"
     D. "What point is the author making about the topic?"

4. The details in a paragraph that directly support the topic sentence or main idea are

called the __________ supporting details. Other details that only indirectly

support the main idea are called the __________ supporting details.

INSTRUCTIONS: Match the words on the left with the words or statements on the right by writing the appropriate choice in each blank:

_______ 5. General

_______ 6. Specific

_______ 7. Paraphrasing

_______ 8. Outlining

_______ 9. Summarizing

A. Stating the core meaning in your own words

B. Supporting details

C. Expressing the author's main points in your own words

D. Creating an organized list of short phrases or single words that suggest the main points

E. The main idea

INSTRUCTIONS: Read the following passage. Then answer the questions that follow:

The oldest cave paintings that have ever been discovered were found in Southern France and Northern Spain and date back to around 20,000 B.C.E. Because many of these paintings look very realistic, some scholars believe that the prehistoric artists spent countless generations developing their painting techniques before they painted the images that are still visible today.

The artifacts that have been found in these caves suggest that the prehistoric artists used a variety of tools to create their works of art. It seems that the prehistoric artists drew lines with red and yellow rocks. They made paint out of these same rocks ground up and mixed with animal fat. The prehistoric painters used flat bones as palettes, and they made brushes from reeds or bristles. When putting pigments on out-of-reach surfaces, they used a hollow reed cut in half and filled with pigment. They then blew into the reed to make the pigment stick onto the surface of the cave. The artists also used stones to flatten out the surfaces of the caves.

Some of the details in the cave paintings raise interesting questions about the people who painted them. For example, the variety of animals depicted sometimes include mammoths and other extinct species, suggesting how very old the paintings must be. In addition, because many of the paintings don't have anything to do with their neighboring paintings or the wall space, it seems that paintings were made at different times. It could also be that prehistoric artists painted for reasons other than expression. Many scholars believe that these caves were thought of as sacred places and that the paintings on the cavern walls were a form of magic. If the art on the wall was a bison, for example, it might have brought the hunters many bison on their next hunt.

These prehistoric people may indeed have used their creations for reasons which we have not as yet figured out, and perhaps never will. But what seems clear is that these paintings have provided modern people with some insight into the lives of some of our prehistoric ancestors.

_______   10.   Which of the following best states the *topic* of this passage?

    A.   Prehistoric culture
    B.   Prehistoric cave art
    C.   Wall painting
    D.   The role of ancient art

_______   11.   Which of the following sentences from the passage best states its *thesis*?

    A.   But what seems clear is that these paintings have provided modern people with some insight into the lives of some of our prehistoric ancestors.
    B.   These prehistoric people may indeed have used their creations for reasons which we have not as yet figured out, and perhaps never will.
    C.   Because many of these paintings look very realistic, some scholars believe that the prehistoric artists spent countless generations developing their painting techniques before they painted the images that are still visible today.
    D.   The oldest cave paintings that have ever been discovered were found in Southern France and Northern Spain and date back to around 20,000 B.C.E.

_______   12.   Which of the following is the *topic sentence* in the second paragraph?

    A.   The artifacts that have been found in these caves suggest that the prehistoric artists used a variety of tools to create their works of art.
    B.   It seems that the prehistoric artists drew lines with red and yellow rocks. They made paint out of these same rocks ground up and mixed with animal fat.
    C.   The prehistoric painters used flat bones as palettes, and they made brushes from reeds or bristles.
    D.   The artists also used stones to flatten out the surfaces of the caves.

_______   13.   Which of the following sentences from the third paragraph represents a *minor* supporting detail?

    A.   Some of the details in the cave paintings suggest things about the people who painted them.
    B.   For example, the variety of animals depicted sometimes include mammoths and other extinct species, suggesting how very old the paintings must be.
    C.   It could also be that prehistoric artists painted for reasons other than expression.
    D.   Many scholars believe that these caves were thought of as sacred places and that the paintings on the cavern walls were a form of magic.

______   14.   Which of the following best paraphrases this sentence from the passage:

"The prehistoric people may indeed have used their creations for reasons which we have not as yet figured out, and perhaps never will."
A.   Modern scholars can never completely understand what motivated the ancient cave painters.
B.   What motivated the prehistoric cave painters may now be unknown and may never be completely understood.
C.   It is virtually impossible to know now anything about what motivated the prehistoric cave painters.
D.   The prehistoric cave painters were so uncivilized that there is no way for modern people to understand them.

15.   INSTRUCTIONS: The outline and summary that follow are for the preceding passage. Use the lettered choices from the list on the right to complete both the outline of the passage on the left below and the summary that follows. One of the choices is a phrase that sums up the main point of the passage, and the rest are supporting points from the paragraphs:

Thesis: ______________

A.   Oldest known cave paintings

B.   Used a variety of tools

   1.   ______________
      a. for drawing
      b. crushed with animal fat for painting

   2.   Bones as palettes

   3.   ______________

   4.   Hollow reeds to blow pigment

   5.   Stones to flatten wall surface

C.   ___________

   1.   Old enough to depict extinct animals

   2.   ______________

   3.   For more than expression
      a. magic
      b. ___________

A.   Inferences about the painters
B.   Aids in hunting
C.   Colored rocks
D.   Made at different times
E.   Reed or bristle brushes
F.   Insights suggested by cave paintings

16. INSTRUCTIONS: Use the lettered choices from the list below to complete summary
that follows:

    A.   Inferences about the painters
    B.   Aids in hunting
    C.   Colored rocks
    D.   Made at different times
    E.   Reed or bristle brushes
    F.   Insights suggested by cave paintings

We can learn something about prehistoric human culture through __________.
The oldest know cave paintings have been found in Europe. The prehistoric artists
used a variety of tools in their work, including ______both for drawing and when
crushed with animal fat for painting, bones as palettes, ____________, hollow reeds
for blowing pigment, stones for flattening the cave wall surfaces. Some ____________
can be made from the details of the cave paintings. Their age is suggested by the
extinct animals depicted, and their nature suggests that they were created at ______.
Also, they seem to have been used for magical purposes, such as for __________
the animals depicted.

NAME _______________________________________

Chapter 4 Review:
Identifying Organizational Patterns

1. Single words or short phrases that are used to connect specific ideas within a sentence
    or between sentences in a passage are called _______________________ , and the
    overall way that the major supporting ideas are structured within the passage is called
    its _______________________________.

INSTRUCTIONS: Match each type of transition on the left with the transitional words or
                 phrases on the right by writing the appropriate choice in each blank:

_______ 2. Addition

_______ 3. Time order

_______ 4. Location

_______ 5. Definition

_______ 6. Clarification

_______ 7. Emphasis

_______ 8. Classification

_______ 9. Comparison

_______ 10. Contrast

_______ 11. Cause and effect

_______ 12. Illustration

_______ 13. Summary

A. as a result, because, consequently, accordingly, affect, hence, therefore

B. in conclusion, in short, to sum up, in sum, in brief, on the whole

C. for example, for instance, to illustrate, namely, specifically, such as, including

D. and, in addition, also, furthermore, moreover, besides, too

E. evidently, in fact, obviously, indeed, clearly, in other words, of course

F. various, categories, types, fields, ranks, aspects, features, characteristics

G. similarly, likewise, like, in the same way, as, in like manner

H. but, although, however, nevertheless, yet, nonetheless, whereas, contrary to

I. next, finally, after, before, during, previously, subsequently, then, until

J. indeed, in fact, certainly, definitely, without a doubt, unquestionably

K. means, is, or, can be defined as, is the same as, like, refers to

L. above, below, beneath, inside, outside, beyond, behind, in front, on top

INSTRUCTIONS: The sentences in items 14–25 are from a passage about psychology. In each one, fill in the blank with an appropriate transition to reflect the relationship between ideas either within a sentence or between it and the previous sentence. Then indicate in the blank below each sentence the type of transition you have used.

14.   The psychoanalytic approach emphasizes the unconscious aspects of the mind, biological instincts, _________________ early family experiences.

      Type of transition: _________________________________

15.   This perspective stresses that unlearned biological instincts, especially sexual and aggressive impulses, _________________ the way people think, feel, and act.

      Type of transition: _________________________________

16.   These instincts are buried deep _________________________ the unconscious mind.

      Type of transition: _________________________________

17.   _________________ these unconscious instincts are natural, they are often at odds with society's demands.

      Type of transition: _________________________________

18.   _________________, one of society's jobs is to keep these instincts in check.

      Type of transition: _________________________________

19.   _________________ , a child who runs wildly through the neighbors' flowers might be encouraged by her parents to channel her aggressive instincts in some more positive way, such as sports.

      Type of transition: _________________________________

20.   _________________, Sigmund Freud argued that our early relationships with our parents are the chief environmental contributions that shape our personality.

      Type of transition: _________________________________

21.   While psychoanalysis focuses on unconscious drives, another _________________ of psychology called developmental psychology focuses on the emotional, cognitive, and social changes that occur over a person's lifetime.

      Type of transition: _________________________________

22.   Some developmental psychologists believe that both adolescents and adults think

_______________________________ .

     Type of transition: _________________________________

23.   However, other developmental psychologists feel that it is not _________________________ adulthood that individuals consolidate their formal operational thinking.

     Type of transition: _________________________________

24.   Formal operational thinking includes the ability of an individual to not only plan and hypothesize about problems but _________________ to approach them systematically.

     Type of transition: _________________________________

25.   _________________ , most psychologists agree both with Freud's ideas about the unconscious and on the importance of the environment in shaping individuals' mental development.

     Type of transition: _________________________________

INSTRUCTIONS: Match each organizational pattern on the left with a definition on the right by writing the appropriate choice in each blank:

______ 26. Enumeration	A. Describes of a series of steps or stages in a procedure.
______ 27. Classification	B. Attempts to clarify or explain a general topic through specific examples.
______ 28. Chronological Order	C. Describes something by its size or location.
______ 29. Process	D. Portrays events occurring in time sequence.
______ 30. Spatial Order	E. Compares one thing to something different that shares something in common with it.
______ 31. Definition and Example	F. Discusses the reasons for or the results of some occurrence or situation.
______ 32. Clarification through Example	G. Introduces a problem and then offers one or more solutions.
______ 33. Comparison/ Contrast	H. Lists information as a series of facts, ideas, or other details.
______ 34. Analogy	

_______	35. Cause and Effect
_______	36. Problem/Solution

I. Deals with similarities and/or differences between two or more things.

J. Explains the meaning of a word or concept through examples.

K. Lists categories, divisions, parts, elements, or types of something.

INSTRUCTIONS: For items 37–47, write in each blank what seems to be the dominant pattern of organization for each of the short passages that follow:

37.   _______________________________________

Every year diseases take many more lives than all the wars and crime combined. By far the most common type of diseases are infectious diseases. All other diseases come under the heading of noninfectious diseases.

38.   _______________________________________

Noninfectious diseases can result from substances that are harmful to the body, such as tobacco smoke or carbon monoxide from automobile exhaust, or from a poor diet. Stress, worry, and the aging process itself are also thought to cause some diseases. Infectious diseases are those that are spread by bacteria, viruses, and other microscopic pathogens commonly called "germs."

39.   _______________________________________

A disease caused by pathogens can be thought of as like a colonial power, whose goal is to enter an unprotected area and establish a settlement. Once one colony is established, especially if there is insufficient resistance from the locals, the colonialists expand their settlements as much as they can. The ultimate goal is to take over the invaded area.

40.   _______________________________________

Some infectious diseases occur mainly in certain climates or geographical areas. For example, African sleeping sickness is almost exclusively found in the hot, humid areas of the continent that gives it its name, where the _tsetse_ fly that carries it lives. Malaria is most often contacted by people who live near swampy areas where certain kinds of mosquitoes breed.

41. ___________________________

One of the most important discoveries in modern medicine occurred in the nineteenth century when Louis Pasteur discovered that immunity to an infectious disease can be induced through a vaccination, the deliberate injection of a weakened or dead bacterium into a patient. Many twentieth century scientists have applied Pasteur's discovery to prevent or cure diseases. One of the most significant examples of the use of a vaccination occurred in the 1950s when Jonas Salk developed the first effective vaccine for poliomyelitis.

42. ___________________________

Both the original discovery by Pasteur and subsequent developments such as Salk's have had extremely significant impacts on society: they have made people feel safer from formerly debilitating and fatal diseases; they have saved many lives; and they have helped encourage other scientists to continue the search for cures for other diseases.

43. ___________________________

The dreaded rabies is contracted by humans from being bitten by an infected animal. The disease travels through the blood stream, with symptoms not occurring until months later. The symptoms of rabies begin with pain or burning numbness where the victim had been bitten, muscle spasms that cause the inability to swallow, headaches, restlessness, convulsions, and then unconsciousness. Finally, if untreated, rabies always causes victims to die horrible, agonizing deaths.

44. ___________________________

Beginning in 1882, Pasteur had been trying to find a vaccine for rabies as proof for his theory that human diseases are caused by pathogens. Then in 1885, a child bitten by a rabid dog was brought by his parents to Pasteur. After several weeks of treatment, the boy never contracted rabies. Pasteur thus proved that a vaccine could indeed cure a serious disease.

45. ___________________________

Polio epidemics had began in the late nineteenth century, but by the early twentieth century, it had reached truly crisis proportion. In 1916, of the 27,000 polio victims in the United States, 6,000 died. Frightened parents were constantly worried that their children would get the disease. In the summer time, parents would keep their children indoors and away from public places and crowds where it was feared they might contact the dreaded illness. Indeed, no one knew what caused it or where it would strike next. These epidemics were ironically caused by improved sanitary standards that prevented young children from developing immunities early in life. By 1949, there were 43,000 cases of poliomyelitis in the United States alone. But by 1954, because of Salk's vaccination, 1,830,000 children had been protected from getting the disease, many of whom would have died without the vaccine.

46.   ______________________________________

Pasteur's discovery of the bacterial nature of many diseases and the use of vaccines as cures had enormous influence on other medical researchers of his time. One such scientist was Robert Koch. Because of the influence of Pasteur's work, Koch was able to find the cause of the White Plague and develop a cure for the disease.

47.   ______________________________________

Like Pasteur, Salk has also influenced many scientists. The most significant influence that Salk made was on Albert B. Sabin. Sabin followed Salk's lead in finding a vaccine to cure polio. However, Sabin's cure was easier to administer. Instead of getting the vaccine through injections, Sabin gave the vaccine in a glass of water or sugar cube that could be taken orally.

INSTRUCTIONS: Write the word in each blank below that best completes the statement by using one of the three words that follow:

general

specific

importance

48.   Sometimes a passage proceeds from a _____________________ main idea to the

_____________________ details. In other situations an author begins with the details

and ends with the main idea. In this case, the author has gone from _______________

to_________________.   You will also often see authors use a rhetorical technique

called order of _____________, in which the point the author wants the reader to

remember most will be emphasized by either locating it first, followed by lesser points,

or by placing it last , preceded by lesser points.

The manner in which stereotyping could work in educational settings was portrayed in a clever third-grade classroom demonstration documented in the film *Eye of the Storm* (1970). Jane Elliot told her students that scientific research had demonstrated that blue-eyed children are smarter than brown-eyed children. She offered a plausible reason why this finding might be true and then offered special privileges to the blue-eyed children while she ridiculed the brown-eyed children. Very soon, she discovered that an in-group and an out-group formed, each making negative comments about the other. Before things got out of control, she interrupted her regular activities again and told the students that she had misinterpreted the finding; she claimed that scientists had actually discovered that brown-eyed children were smarter. Again, she offered a justification and resumed giving differential treatment. The same stereotyping occurred again. She concluded the experiment and revealed the nature of her deception, followed by a frank talk about the stereotypes that had formed and the behaviors that developed as a consequence. Like the experience in Jane Elliot's class, many students can describe some academic challenges that they attribute to stereotyping and the prejudicial behavior that followed.

Jane S. Hallonen & John W. Santock,
Psychology: Contexts of Behavior

49.   This passage begins and ends with __________.

    A. general statements of the main idea.
    B. supporting details.
    C. the most important details.

50.   This main pattern of organization used in this passage is __________.

    A. chronological order.
    B. analogy.
    C. cause and effect.

NAME ________________________________

Chapter 5 Review:
Using Inference

1. INSTRUCTIONS: Choose from the following words to fill in the blanks in the
    sentences below:

    inference
    drawing conclusions
    purpose
    tone

When you are using your knowledge, experience, logic, and awareness of techniques

of writing to interpret meanings that go beyond an author's literal statements, you are

using ________________________. When doing so to determine implications,

consequences, or courses of action from the details of an author's discussion, you are

________________________________. You also use this ability whenever you are

trying to recognize an author's reason for writing, or his or her ______________, and

the attitude with which they write, or the author's ____________________.

---

2. INSTRUCTIONS: Choose from the following words identifying different purposes
    for writing to fill in the three blanks in the sentences below:

    entertain
    inform
    persuade

If the writing is meant to explain or instruct, to tell readers about something, or

to present information clearly so readers can understand it as easily as possible, its

purpose is to ____________________. Writing that is meant to convince readers to

believe in some idea or to influence them to take some course of action is meant to

________________. Writing that amuses or provides readers with an enjoyable

experience is intended to ____________________.

---

3. The tone of a passage can often be inferred from the author's choice of ______________
    and from the way that ________________ are discussed and presented.

INSTRUCTIONS: Read the following excerpt from an article about recent research findings suggesting that both hostile and nurturing behavior involve complex physical changes in the body that make the behavior possible. After reading the passage, answer the questions that follow, requiring you to make inferences and draw conclusions:

The warrior's so-called stress circuitry is indicated and labeled. The levels of fight-or-flight hormones like cortisol and epinephrine are surging, his heart rate has accelerated, his blood pressure and blood sugar are soaring, and any gastrointestinal activity that could divert energy from his muscles has ceased. All in all, he is in a state of physiological catabolism, a mobilization and breaking down of the body's energy stores for the business of attacking an enemy.

Of the calm Madonna circuitry—the physical condition that defines a woman who is nurturing her baby—comparatively less is known, Dr. Uvnas-Moberg said, but researchers are beginning to flesh out the details. In a lactating woman, anabolism replaces catabolism: the emphasis is on building up rather than tearing apart. Insulin levels mount, the better to pull sugar from the blood and store it in cells; so, too, do the concentrations of gastric acids and hormones like gastrin and cholecystokinin, all of which aid in efficient digestion and the transfer of energy from food to the body and to breast milk.

Within minutes after beginning a bout of nursing, the mother's cortisol levels subside and her blood pressure drops, fostering a sense of relaxation that keeps her willingly quiescent for as long as it takes to sate her child; at the same time, the blood vessels of her chest dilate, which turns her into a living space heater to warm the suckling infant.

If the fight-or-flight response is seen as a strengthening of the distinction between self and the other—a tightening of the body's response mechanisms, like springs compressed into a box—then the affiliative, nurturing circuitry suggests an opening up, an expansion of self toward others, and a trading of anxiety for at least a momentary state of quiet joy.

Natalie Angier, "Illuminating How Our Bodies are Built for Sociability"

_______   4. From what is said in the first paragraph, it seems that the hormones cortisol and epinephrine are associated with

     A. normal bodily functions.
     B. violent action.
     C. athletic competition.
     D. male behavior.

_______   5. By saying in the second paragraph that "researchers are beginning to flesh out the details," the author is implying that

     A. a lot of research is presently going on.
     B. a lot of research has already been done.
     C. relatively little research has been done in the past.
     D. scientists are on the verge a significant discovery.

______   6. In the third paragraph, the author describes the physiological processes active when a woman nurses a baby. The author implies that these processes

A. leave the mother feeling drained.
B. are mostly deliberate.
C. are triggered by the mother's feeling of love for her child.
D. contribute to the mother's desire to continue nursing.

______   7. In the fourth paragraph, the author implies that both the "fight-or-flight response" experienced by someone in battle and the "momentary state of quiet joy" that a mother feels when nursing her baby are

A. similar physiological responses.
B. different responses to similar situations.
C. only mental states.
D. opposite responses.

______   8. After reading this passage, it seems that the research the author is describing suggests that a woman's nursing capacity is mostly

A. genetic.
B. learned.
C. dependent upon physiological processes.
D. independent of physiological processes.

______   9. The research described by the author also suggests that nursing is

A. not automatic.
B. a pleasant experience for women.
C. made possible by the woman's mental state.
D. unnecessary.

______   10. A conclusion that can be drawn from this passage is that both fighting and nurturing behavior

A. require hormonal and other physiological responses.
B. are triggered by emotional states.
C. are the defining characteristics of men and women respectively.
D. occur quite commonly.

______   11. It thus seems that both violent aggression and nursing are

A. common.
B. learned.
C. desirable.
D. natural.

INSTRUCTIONS: From the following choices, identify the purpose and tone for each of the passages below. You will find at least one example of each purpose but just one example of each tone:

<u>Purposes</u>   <u>Tones</u>

Entertain   Critical   Ironic   Pessimistic
Inform   Impassioned   Objective   Respectful
Persuade   Indignant   Optimistic   Sarcastic
                                           Tragic

12. Purpose: ________________________   Tone: ________________________

The aesthetic aspect of the Plains shield is pronounced; the shield is a unique work of art. Without exception great care is given to the decoration of a proper shield. The artwork on many Plains shields is highly evolved in terms of proportion, design, symmetry, color, and imagination. Plains shield art is the equal of the great ledgerbook drawings of the nineteenth century, which in turn have been compared to Archaic Greek vase painting. It is an art of high order and singular accomplishment.

N. Scott Momaday, *In the Presence of the Sun*

13. Purpose: ________________________   Tone: ________________________

"Just as she turned her head away from the windows, the room was filled with a blinding light. She was paralyzed with fear, fixed in her chair for a long moment (the plant was 1,600 yards from the center).

"Everything fell, and Miss Sasaki lost consciousness. The ceiling dropped suddenly and the wooden floor above collapsed in splinters and the people up there came down and the roof gave way; but principally and first of all, the bookcases right behind her swooped forward and the contents threw her down, with her left leg horribly twisted and breaking underneath her. There, in the tin factory, in the first moment of the atomic age, a human being was crushed by books."

John Hirsey, *Hiroshima*

14. Purpose: ________________________   Tone: ________________________

We live in an age that strives for easy digestion. Cough syrup comes in gel caps. Political candidates speak in 8-second bites. "War and Peace" comes on audiotape. Some things, though, are not improved in the quest for convenience. Consider this: "But wait! What light is coming from that window?"

Sound vaguely familiar? It is poetry de-poeticized. Here now is the glorious original: "But soft! What light through yonder window breaks?"

Harcourt Brace & Company

In both cases, Romeo idealizes Juliet who stands on her balcony. But only in the second do the words belong to Shakespeare. The first is from a parallel text edition of "Romeo and Juliet." For students, the works of Shakespeare have been trimmed and translated into what one text calls "a neutral and comprehensible modern equivalent."

Peter Marks, "Translations of the
Bard:Perorations Devoutly to be Missed"

15. Purpose: _______________________   Tone: _______________________

As sight, hearing, and even the ability of the correspondents to write diminished, the letters between Adams and Jefferson dwindled to a trickle. Somehow, without perhaps even consciously willing it, they concentrated their enfeebled energies on surviving until the coming Fourth of July, 1826, which would mark the fiftieth anniversary of independence. By whatever amiable intervention of Providence, the two old friends both died on that hallowed day. . . . Now, while their fellow citizens celebrated the day in every city and town, the two heroes of the Revolution died. Adams's last words were, "Jefferson still lives," but Jefferson had, in fact, died several hours earlier.

Page Smith, *The Shaping of America*

16. Purpose: _______________________   Tone: _______________________

Veterans of previous outbreaks of technological euphoria, though, are skeptical. "Each time a new medium comes along, great hopes are raised," said Erik Barnouw, a professor emeritus at Columbia University and a media historian. "But the lesson of history is that every new medium provides new opportunities for selling as well as for education, for monopolists as well as for democracy, and for abuse as well as for benefit."

Steve Lohr, "The Great Unplugged Masses
Confront the Future"

17. Purpose: _______________________   Tone: _______________________

Imagine if everybody had a computer for $9,000 and you were stuck by a table every time you had to learn anything or read anything . . . And all of a sudden somebody invented a whole new thing—a newspaper! You know what would happen? Everybody would say, "What an invention! A newspaper! For half a dollar you got the same thing!" Not only that, you can take it wherever you want to go. You can't take a computer to the toilet. . . . You can take this wherever you want—wherever you want! The dog: he's about to go—do you put a computer underneath?

Jackie Mason, "Taking a P.C. to the Toilet"

18.   Purpose: ________________________   Tone: ________________________

Joe Montana is the greatest quarterback ever. Dan Marino owns a lot of impressive numbers but not the one that defines his position best. That .715 career winning percentage, best of any QB in NFL history, belongs to Montana. Maybe Marino is a better *passer* than Montana, but he is not a better quarterback.

Passing yardage? TD passes? It's nice but meaningless. You don't measure a quarterback by individual stats. You don't measure his worth with things like "quick release" any more than you measure Rembrandt by the way he dipped his brush. You measure a quarterback by how much he wins, and Joe Montana has won four Super Bowls. Marino has won none.

> Dan Le Batard, "No! It's Joe: Sorry—The Rings Say It All"

19.   Purpose: ________________________   Tone: ________________________

When I looked outside right into the depth of Nature and God, then I was happy, really happy. And Peter, so long as I have that happiness here, the joy in nature, health, and a lot more besides, all the while one has that, one can always recapture happiness.

> Anne Frank, *The Diary of a Young Girl*

20.   Purpose: ________________________   Tone: ________________________

We have found that the even distribution of happiness cuts across almost all demographic classifications of age, economic class, race and educational level. In addition, almost all strategies for assessing subjective well-being--including those that sample people's experience by polling them at random times with beepers—turn up similar findings.

Interviews with representative samples of people of all ages, for example, reveal that no time of life is notably happier or unhappier. Similarly, men and women are equally likely to declare themselves "very happy" and "satisfied" with life, according to a statistical digest of 146 studies by Marilyn J. Haring, William Stock and Morris A. Okun, all then at Arizona State University. Alex Michalos of the University of Northern British Columbia and Ronald Inglehart of the University of Michigan, summarizing newer surveys of 18,000 university students in 39 countries and 170,000 adults in 16 countries, corroborate these findings.

> David G. Myers and Ed Diener "The Pursuit of Happiness"

Chapter 6 Review:

Interpreting Language

---

1. Every word has a literal, dictionary definition, which is called its ________________ .

   On the other hand, a word's emotional or suggestive is called its ________________ .

INSTRUCTIONS: Match each type of figurative expression on the left with its definition on the right by writing the appropriate choice in each blank:

_______ 2. Euphemism

_______ 3. Idiom

_______ 4. Simile

_______ 5. Metaphor

_______ 6. Hyperbole

_______ 7. Personification

_______ 8. Symbolism

_______ 9. Irony

A. A commonly used expression composed of words whose meanings differ from their usual definitions.

B. An implied comparison, when two unlike things are spoken of as if they were actually the same.

C. An attribution of human characteristics to nonhuman things or concepts.

D. A polite-sounding word used to soften the effect of a harsh, sensitive, embarrassing, or unpleasant reality.

E. The use of a recognizable, easily understood image to stand for, epitomize, encapsulate, or represent something else.

F. The use of words whose literal meanings are the opposite of what is really meant.

G. An overstatement that seems stronger or more extravagant than the situation calls for but that is used to make a point.

H.   A figurative expression that directly compares two unlike things sharing some common quality.

INSTRUCTIONS: Identify the connotations of the underlined words in the following sentences by writing either "positive" or "negative" in each blank:

10.   ________________________

His <u>trusting</u> nature is quite remarkable, considering what he has been through.

11.   ________________________

No matter how people treat him, he remains remarkably <u>gullible</u>.

12.   ________________________

Her <u>aggressive</u> personality made her many friends and enemies.

13.   ________________________

Her <u>ambitious</u> nature has led her to take many risks, many of which have rewarded her with success.

INSTRUCTIONS: The following sentences contain underlined euphemisms and idioms. Answer the questions that follow each sentence concerning the meaning of each euphemism or idiom:

________   14.   Your son <u>seems to require constant reminders to focus on his work</u>.
This statement is a euphemism meaning that the son is

    A. bad.
    B. clumsy.
    C. unintelligent.
    D. lazy.

________   15.   You have just <u>shown an inability to distinguish between imaginary and factual information</u>.
This is a euphemism meaning that the person spoken to has

    A. lied.
    B. made a mistake.
    C. exaggerated.
    D. forgotten something.

______   16.   I <u>ran into</u> an old friend yesterday at the supermarket.
         This idiom means that the writer

    A. collided with someone.
    B. introduced himself to someone.
    C. met someone he knew.
    D. was running in the supermarket aisles.

______   17.   After waiting for an hour at the restaurant, I left after concluding that he had
         <u>stood me up</u>.
         This idiom means that the person the writer had been waiting for

    A. did not meet her after promising that he would.
    B. stood up suddenly from his chair.
    C. arrived early and then left before she arrived.
    D. had innocently forgotten about the engagement.

INSTRUCTIONS: From the following choices, identify the type of figurative expression
underlined in the passages. For each figurative expression underlined
in a passage, write in the type of expression in the space to the left. You
will use each choice at least once:

Hyperbole	Metaphor	Simile
Idiom	Personification	Symbolism
Irony		

18. ____________________

19. ____________________

20. ____________________

21. ____________________

22. ____________________

No one ever understood my wild and secret ways.
They used to say <u>Lulu Lamarine was like a cat,
loving on one, only purring to get what she
wanted</u>. But that's not true. I was in love with the
whole world and all that lived in <u>its rainy arms</u>.
Sometimes I'd look out on my yard and <u>the green
leaves would be glowing</u>. I'd hear the <u>wind
rushing, rolling, like the far-off sound of
waterfalls</u>. Then I'd open my mouth wide, my ears
wide, my heart, and <u>I'd let everything inside.</u>

Louise Erdrich, *Love Medicine*

23. _________________

If you're a close listener, you'll notice that the buzz from the big-eared billionaire's corner has keened into a higher pitch. Not because the lumpen Joes are demanding to be heard this election season, but because they've been drowned out by their equally disgruntled better halves: the angry white females, America's hottest new swing vote. "Every poll shows that, regardless of where

24. _________________

25. _________________

they come from, less-educated blue-collar women are the largest group of volatile voters," says Mary

26. _________________

Beth Cahill of Emily's List, whose members are

27. _________________

more likely to have blue hair than blue collars. "We've become convinced that winning them

28. _________________

over is the key to Democratic fortunes."

Hanna Rosin, "Working Girls"

My wife and I are not the sort of people who make a big deal out of our tax returns. As far as we're concerned it's just another rite of spring that has to be dealt with, like spreading mulch on the lawn and manure in the rose garden.

29. _________________

Not long ago, as we have done for so many years, we cleared off the dining room table, sat down with all our forms, the checkbook, a bottle of champagne and two classes, donned funny paper

30. _________________

hats, and went to work.

Art Buchwald, You <u>Can</u> Fool All of the People All the Time

Chapter 7 Review:
Reading Literature

INSTRUCTIONS: Match the types of writing on the left with their definitions on the right by writing the appropriate choices in the blanks:

_______   1. Literature

_______   2. Prose

_______   3. Poetry

_______   4. Exposition

_______   5. Persuasion/Argumentation

_______   6. Description

_______   7. Narration

_______   8. Essay

_______   9. Autobiography

_______   10. Nonfiction

_______   11. Fiction

A. Showing what something or someone looks like or feels like by creating a sensory image or a mental picture with words.

B. Writing that portrays actual events, persons, or issues.

C. Writing intended to inform, explain, or instruct.

D. Language used in continuous sentences and paragraphs.

E. Relating events in the form of a story, taken either from real life or from an author's imagination.

F. Attempts to influence readers' beliefs or actions concerning some idea or issue.

G. Written expression dealing with human experience in finely crafted, artistic works.

H. A composition discussing a specific topic in a few paragraphs, a few pages, or an entire book.

I. Stories that come from an author's imagination rather than from facts or actual people or events.

Harcourt Brace & Company

J.   Recounting events from an author's life as a way to point out personal or cultural significance.

K.   A form of literary expression involving condensed language with words chosen for their sound and suggesting power.

INSTRUCTIONS: Each of the following short passages represents a different mode of expression or type of literary nonfiction. Indicate which type of writing each passage is by writing one of the letters below in each blank. Use each choice only once. Notice that one passage requires two answer choices, one that identifies its mode of expression and one for its type of literary nonfiction:

<u>Modes of Expression</u>   <u>Types of Literary Nonfiction</u>

A. Exposition   E. The Essay

B. Persuasion/Argumentation   F. Autobiography

C. Description

D. Narration

_______ 12.   It was on 98th Street, across from the tall long sinister stone wall on which the Third Avenue El trains came to rest, that I began to know I would never get to America. Though I learned in the kindergarten on 96th Street, among the many other English words that I taught my brother with a prissy, powerful passion, that I lived in America, it was not the America promised me in Warsaw or by the chocolate sweetness of my father's mouth. There were no sacks of candy and cookies, no dolls, no perennial summer that meant America. America was a stern man whose duty it was to cure us of being the cosseted spoiled little beasts our mother and her idiot sisters had allowed to flourish. . . .

Kate Simon, *Bronx Primitive*

_______ 13.   For most of the people on this fertile coast, most of "The West" is, as people like to say, Back East. It belongs to the past. It is where parents and grandparents lived and—mostly—failed, leaving a forlorn trail of abandoned homesteads, bankrupt businesses, exhausted mines, and empty logging camps behind them.

_______ 14.   Serial failure is the driving theme in the family narratives of a great many of my immediate neighbors: high hopes dashed, rekindled, dashed again, as families crawled westward, in meagre increments of a hundred miles or so, until at last they found a modestly secure anchorage somewhere between the Cascades and the Pacific.

Jonathan Raban, "The Unlamented West"

_______ 15.   Maycomb was an old town, but it was a tired old town when I first knew it. In rainy weather the streets turned to red slop; grass grew on the sidewalks, the courthouse sagged in the square. Somehow, it was hotter then: a black dog suffered on a summer day; bony mules hitched to Hoover carts flicked flies in the sweltering shade of the live oaks on the square. Men's stiff collars wilted by nine in the morning. Ladies bathed before noon, after their three-o'clock naps, and by nightfall were like soft teacakes with frostings of sweat and sweet talcum.

Harper Lee, *To Kill a Mockingbird*

_______ 16.   At the sound of the twist of my shoe in the gravel, the young woman's whole body was jerked down tight as a fist into a crouch from which immediately, the rear foot skidding in the loose stone so that she nearly fell, like a kicked cow scrambling out of a creek, eyes crazy, chin stretched tight, she sprang forward into the first motions of a running not human but that of a suddenly terrified wild animal.

James Agee, *Let Us Now Praise Famous Men*

_______ 17.   At the risk of being branded some kind of moral monster who favors parental irresponsibility, beats up on the beleaguered two-parent family, and spits in the face of common sense, I want to argue that the revival of the family values crusade poses serious dangers for people who sincerely want to improve the lives of American children. *Of course* values are important, and *of course* there are some truly awful parental behaviors and family dynamics out there. But polarizing the issues as *their* bad values or *their* bad parents versus our commitment to kids ignores the fact that *all* of *us* have bad values as well as good ones.

Stephanie Coontz, "The American Family and the Nostalgia Trap"

INSTRUCTIONS: Complete the following sentences with the words from the list below that identify the different elements of fiction:

Characters	Point of View
Effect	Setting
Plot	Theme

18.   A story's ___________________ includes the time, place, and circumstances in which it happens.

19.   The ___________________ are the people (or animals, as the case may be) depicted in the story.

20. The ___________________ consists of the events that take place in the story and the meaning that they events have.

21. The perspective from which a story is told is called its ___________________.

22. The ___________________ of a story is its central meaning or the main point.

23. In a fictional work, the impression or impact the story has on readers is referred to as its

___________________.

INSTRUCTIONS: Read the following excerpt from a short story. Then answer the questions that follow:

    The city pool was full of children that day, but I don't think that's what bothered me. I was fourteen and happy to be out with my friends. It was sunny but cool for mid-July in Iowa. A breeze flipped up the edges of our beach towels as we lined them up on the crumbling cement, anchoring them with clogs, a bottle of coconut oil, and a transistor radio that seemed to play nothing but Sammy Davis Jr. singing "The Candy Man." My friends flopped down on their backs and fell asleep, but I couldn't relax. I sat cross-legged in my faded bikini, a hand-me-down from my sister, Daisy.
    Daisy was lifeguarding, but she couldn't see me, didn't even know I was there. She looked like a stranger, perched above the masses in her red tank suit and mirror sunglasses, her nose a triangle of zinc oxide. In one month she was going away to college, leaving me to take care of our father. I couldn't let myself think about how dreary life would be without Daisy. I gazed out at the pool, which was circular, with the deep part and diving island in the center. A group of four or five children splashed around at the edge of the deep water, shrieking and dunking one another. A smaller girl in a green one-piece bathing suit dog-paddled near the splashers, barely keeping her chin above water. She wanted to play too, but the other children—friends? neighbors? sisters and brothers?—ignored her. Teenagers were doing cannonballs off the high board, and their waves sloshed over her head. Nobody except me seemed to notice. The girl was paddling as hard as she could, getting nowhere.

Elizabeth Stuckey-French, "Junior"

_______ 24.   This narrator of this story is

    A. omniscient.
    B. a teen-aged girl who is remembering the past.
    C. Daisy's best friend.
    D. the author who is describing an experience from her life.

_______   25.   It also seems that the narrator is

  A. going to be an important character in the story.
  B. probably not going to play an important role in the story.
  C. going to do something important with Daisy.
  D. going to play with the little girl in the pool.

_______   26.   This part of the story seems to take place

  A. around a swimming pool at an indeterminate time.
  B. in Iowa, probably in the 1960's.
  C. at a swimming pool in Iowa, probably in the 1990's.
  D. somewhere that readers cannot determine.

_______   27.   It seems likely that the plot of this story will develop according to something that

  A. Daisy will do with her sister.
  B. the little girl in the pool will do.
  C. the kids at the pool will do to the narrator.
  D. will happen at the pool.

_______   28.   From this excerpt, it seems likely that the theme of this story will have something to do with

  A. life in the Midwest.
  B. aquatic sports.
  C. academic learning.
  D. growing up.

_______   29.   This passage seems to evoke a mood of

  A. happiness.
  B. restlessness.
  C. loneliness.
  D. compassion.

INSTRUCTIONS: Complete the following sentences with the words from the list below that identify the different elements of poetry:

<u>Arrangement</u>	<u>Content</u>
Free Verse	Effect
Rhyme	Emotion
Rhythm	Imagery
	Significance

30.   The regular flow produced by the sound of carefully chosen words in a poem is called
its ___________________.

31.   If the ends of two or more lines have the same or a very similar sound, the poem is
said to have ___________________.

32.   ___________________ refers to poetry that is based on irregular rhythms and that
may or may not rhyme at all.

33.   The expression of feelings in a poem is known as its ___________________.

34.   Poems often use figurative language to suggest human emotions, understanding, and
experience through ___________________.

35.   The ___________________ of a poem lies in its topic and the way it tries to
interpret human experience and broaden understanding.

36.   The overall ___________________ of a poem is in how well it evokes in readers a
powerful experience, such as of beauty, shame, pain, joy, inspiration, or peace.

INSTRUCTIONS: Read the excerpt below from a very well-known poem by Elizabeth
Barrett Browning. Then answer the questions that follow:

> How do I love thee? Let me count the ways.
> I love thee to the depth and breadth and height
> My soul can reach, when feeling out of sight
> For the ends of Being and ideal Grace.
> I love thee to the level of everyday's
> Most quiet need, by sun and candlelight.

Elizabeth Barrett Browning,
Sonnets from the Portuguese

_______ 37.   This poem uses an arrangement that

A. is known as free verse.
B. incorporates both rhythm and rhyme.

_______ 38.   In this poem, Browning is expressing feelings of

A. despair.
B. longing.
C. love.
D. compassion.

_______ 39.   When Browning refers to "sun and candlelight," she means

A. natural and artificial light.
B. happiness and sadness.
C. life and death.
D. day and night.

_______ 40.   The human experience portrayed in this poem is

A. religious devotion.
B. the longing for love.
C. romantic love.
D. spiritual peace.

Chapter 8 Review:
Recognizing Persuasive Writing

INSTRUCTIONS: Complete the following sentences with the words from the list below:

Bias   Slanting
Fact   Value Words
Opinion   Weasel Words

1.   Something that can be objectively verified or proven in some way is called a(n)

_______________________.

2.   On the other hand, a(n) _______________ is something that expresses a view toward
something that cannot be verified or proven in any way.

3.   Whenever an author makes a prediction about the future, he or she is expressing a(n)

_______________________.

4.   Words that express a positive or negative view of something are called

_______________________and indicate that a(n) _______________is being expressed.

5.   Words chosen for their emotional effect in an attempt to persuade readers that

something is true without any proof are called _______________________.

6.   Deliberately misrepresenting something by creating either a positive or negative

impression as if there were no other way of looking at the issue is called

_______________________.

7.   An author's attitude or prejudice that influences his or her perspective on a subject is

called the author's _______________________.

INSTRUCTIONS: The following sentences are from a newspaper article (Gina Kolata, "The Unwholesome Tale of the Herb Market," the *New York Times*, April 21, 1996, page 6E). Indicate whether each sentence states a fact, an opinion, or both fact and opinion by circling your choice on the left. Then if you notice any value words in a sentence, write them in the space to the right; if not, leave the space blank:

8.   Fact   Opinion   Fact/Opinion   Value Words: _________________________________

Some people assume that what is natural is good for you, or at least harmless. That assumption, as it turns out, is a great marketing ploy but a dangerous motto for living.

9.   Fact   Opinion   Fact/Opinion   Value Words: _________________________________

Not all dietary supplements are dangerous, of course. In many cases, the worst that happens is that people waste their money.

10.   Fact   Opinion   Fact/Opinion   Value Words: _________________________________

Less than three years ago, tens of thousands of Americans, responding to an intense lobbying campaign by the food supplement industry, wrote, faxed and telephoned members of Congress, urging them to deregulate the industry.

11.   Fact   Opinion   Fact/Opinion   Value Words: _________________________________

Mitchell Zeller, the deputy associate commissioner for policy at the FDA, who was, at the time, a congressional staffer, said that Congress received more mail in 1993 urging it to deregulate supplements than it received on any other issue that year, including health care reform or NAFTA.

INSTRUCTIONS: Read the following excerpt from the same newspaper article. Then answer the questions that follow:

So far, at least 15 people have died in the United States after taking herbal products containing ephedrine, also known as ephedra or ma huang. And yet, this herbal drug is still on the market along with other untested herbs and so-called food supplements, including vitamins, amino acids, melatonin and "natural" birth control pills from yams.

Richard Friedman, a psychiatrist who directs the Psychopharmacology Clinic at New York Hospital–Cornell Medical Center, wanted to test the limits on what kinds of herbs could be sold without approval from the Food and Drug Administration.

So he called the FDA. Suppose, he asked, he wanted to sell hemlock tea, the deadly poison that Socrates drank. Would there be any way for the FDA to stop him before his tea was on the shelves in health food stores and groceries across the nation? The answer was no.

The FDA, he learned, "couldn't stop me from selling hemlock tea until the bodies piled up."

Gina Kolata, "The Unwholesome Tale of the Herb Market"

___________ 12.   The first paragraph above mostly contains

   A.   facts.
   B.   opinions.
   C.   weasel words.
   D.   value words.

___________ 13.   However, the expression "so-called" used in the first sentence in reference to food supplements indicates that the author

   A.   does not know what they should really be called.
   B.   thinks many of them are not legitimate.
   C.   does not like to take vitamins.
   D.   thinks they should probably be illegal.

___________ 14.   Also, by using quotation marks around the word "natural" the author is probably suggesting that products such as birth control pills made from yams

   A.   are actually derived from natural sources.
   B.   are more healthy then artificial products.
   C.   may not really be as natural as a consumer would like to think.
   D.   may be less effective than artificial products.

___________ 15.   In the last paragraph, Dr. Richard Friedman uses the phrase "until the bodies piled up" to

   A.   express his outrage over the misuse of hemlock.
   B.   show his fear of what may happen if hemlock is not regulated.
   C.   make the FDA seem dangerously ineffective.
   D.   predict the consequences of excessive government regulation.

___________ 16.   Dr. Friedman seems to have a bias

   A.   against excessive governmental regulation.
   B.   in favor of government regulation of herbal supplements.
   C.   against herbal supplements.
   D.   in favor of herbal products such as hemlock tea.

INSTRUCTIONS: Each of the following sentences represents a different logical fallacy. Indicate the type of fallacy by writing a letter in each blank:

Logical Fallacies with Irrelevant Support

    A.   Non Sequitur

    B.   Two Wrongs Make a Right

    C.   Red Herring

_______ 17.   The editors of the *Tribune* have no right to criticize Senator Sneed for voting in favor of legislation that benefits those who have so generously contributed to his reelection campaign, when they themselves headline sensational stories for no other reason than to sell papers.

_______ 18.   If you would like more pizza, we would be happy to cut yours into eight pieces instead of six.

_______ 19.   The Panthers should be disqualified from the championship series because every time they score a goal, their fans throw rubber rats onto the rink, which disrupts and delays the game.

Logical Fallacies with Insufficient Support

A.	Hasty Generalization	E.	Appeal to Ignorance
B.	False Cause	F.	Begging the Question
C.	False Comparison	G.	Circular Reasoning
D.	False Dilemma	H.	Stacked Evidence

_______ 20.   Either kids are taught to use computers or they will be consigned to flipping hamburgers for the rest of their lives.

_______ 21.   We need to increase military expenditures because more money is needed for defense.

_______ 22.   The decrease of Spanish-language competency in South Florida is inevitable, for their situation is not unlike that of all other non–English speaking immigrant groups throughout the history of this country. Take the case of German immigrants. In 1910, there were over 500 German-language publications in the United States. However, by the time of the 1990 census, only about 3 percent of those people claiming German ancestry still spoke German at home. We will surely see the same phenomena with Hispanic-Americans in the twenty-first century.

_______ 23. The lack of conclusive evidence suggesting the senator's guilt proves that he is innocent of any improprieties.

_______ 24. It was not long after the NAFTA agreement was passed that the Mexican economy took a dive. I knew that treaty would result in serious economic problems.

_______ 25. The tobacco industry cannot be blamed for respiratory problems such as lung cancer and emphysema when research clearly suggests that air pollution is a major cause of such illnesses.

_______ 26. I've learned what liberals believe from talking to my neighbor who thinks the government can solve every social problem.

_______ 27. Abortion is a clearly justifiable right that a woman has to make decisions concerning her own body.

Ethical Fallacies

A.   Argument to the Person

B.   Straw Man

C.   False Use of Authority

_______ 28. Senator Jackson's support for increased trade with China is indefensible, for it shows his tacit support for the Chinese government's brutal treatment of the Tibetans and toward the leaders of the democracy movement.

_______ 29. As a well-respected researcher who has published several highly regarded books in his field, Professor Siegler's assessment of the quality of teaching in this university should be taken more seriously than other professors who do not have as respectable a scholarly record.

_______ 30. The fact that Janet Miller is a divorced woman who has never had children suggests that she certainly would not make an effective juvenile court judge.

Emotional Fallacies

A.   Appeal to the People   D.   False Needs

B.   Appeal to Pity   E.   Glittering Generalities

C.   Bandwagon Appeal   F.   Slippery Slope

_______ 31. Join the millions of other voters who support Henry Hughes for governor. He is obviously the best candidate—the people's choice.

_______ 32. The Liberty Bell Insurance Company now offers a unique credit card insurance policy that protects you from unauthorized charges in the event that your card is ever lost or stolen. In a society where crime is unfortunately too great a threat, without this policy you are vulnerable in ways you simply cannot afford.

_______ 33. A national health care plan would be just the first step in bringing everything important under the federal government's inefficient control. First, it would be health insurance; then it would be education; soon nothing would be left to local or private discretion.

_______ 34. Imagine a life free of financial worry. If you think this an unattainable goal, then you have not heard of the Freedom Fund. More than any other retirement investment plan, Freedom Fund offers the chance for you to invest your dollars in your own future, a future you deserve to enjoy.

_______ 35. Because she is innocent of any deliberate wrong-doing, Ms. Gault deserves our compassion, not our judgment. She obviously didn't leave the office unlocked on purpose, and her computer was stolen along with all the other things taken in the break-in. Her all-to-human error is not reason enough for her to be fired.

_______ 36. The Republican Party offers the only chance for this nation to escape the moral degeneration that more than three decades of Democratic social experimentation have led us into. The results of the Democratic-controlled Congress are all around us—crime, poor schools, drug use, teen-age pregnancy, divorce, lack of respect for authority. We can no longer afford to continue down this road to ruin.

INSTRUCTIONS: Read the following sentences. Then complete the statements that require a critical analysis of the author's persuasive attempts:

_______ 37. "In the past two thousand years, over ten thousand wars have been fought on this planet. Clearly, we are a warlike species."

After reading this, one would probably wonder

A. how the author got these statistics.
B. why this has not been pointed out before.
C. how we have been able to survive so long.
D. why so many wars have been fought.

_______ 38. "If marijuana is legalized for medicinal use, much of its glamour will disappear for teenagers. Since few teenagers dress like their grandparents, what kid would still think it cool to light up a joint, if that's what Grandpa does for his glaucoma?"

Which of the following statements shows why this is an example of a faulty analogy?

A. Kids might steal marijuana cigarettes from their grandparents.
B. Many teenagers smoke tobacco even though some grandparents smoke.
C. Partial legalization of marijuana could eventually lead to full legalization.
D. The recreational use of marijuana by teenagers is on the rise.

_______ 39. "The power of prayer has been demonstrated by the several people who survived the plane crash and stated that they had been praying as the plane went down."

Which of the following is a logical reason to doubt that the author's conclusion
about prayer saving these people is the only possible explanation for their survival?

A. The people could have been lying.
B. Some of the people who were killed may also have been praying.
C. These people might have only believed that prayer saved them.
D. Other people survived who had not been praying.

_______ 40. "The Starcruiser is the most reliable recreational vehicle on the road today."

Who would you take most seriously if they were to make this statement?

A. An employee of the company that manufactures Starcruisers
B. A person who wrote a letter-to-the-editor of a car magazine
C. A reporter for *Consumer Reports* magazine who reviewed the car
D. A movie star in an advertisement who is promoting the car

NAME ________________________________

Chapter 9 Review:
Analyzing Arguments

---

1. A(n) ________________________ is a type of persuasion involving attempts to convince primarily through the use of reasoning and objective evidence and is composed of three parts:

>   the ________________________— the main point the author is trying to prove;

>   the ________________________— evidence provided in an attempt to convince readers to accept the thesis.

>   the ________________________— the generally accepted truths or beliefs underlying the support meant to make the support believable.

INSTRUCTIONS: Match each type of type of claim, appeal, and assumption on the left with its definition on the right by writing the appropriate choice in each blank:

_______ 2. Factual Claim	A. Factual or objective evidence.
_______ 3. Value Claim	B. Based on what most people commonly believe is true.
_______ 4. Logical Appeal	C. Appeals to readers' needs or values.
_______ 5. Ethical Appeal	D. Affirms the existence of something, defines something, or claims something as a cause.
_______ 6. Emotional Appeal	E. Based on beliefs concerning the trustworthiness of a source.
_______ 7. Factual Assumption	F. Passes judgment or expresses approval or disapproval.
_______ 8. Authoritative Assumption	G. Based on what most people believe is important, more important than something else, or most important of all.
_______ 9. Value Assumption	H. Makes the author seem trustworthy.

INSTRUCTIONS: Identify each of the following thesis statements as representing either a factual or a value claim:

10. _____________________ claim

People are not born racists. They learn racist behavior from the environment in which they grow up.

11. _____________________ claim

The most significant problem facing the world today involves the destruction of the natural environment.

12. _____________________ claim

Contrary to popular belief, most of the better-paying jobs that are now being created do not require a four-year college degree.

13. _____________________ claim

Walt Whitman's main contribution to American poetry is in his use of uniquely American themes.

14. _____________________ claim

You can effectively reduce the likelihood that your car will be stolen by always locking your car doors, parking in a safe place, and using protective devices.

15. _____________________ claim

As the first totally computer-animated full-length film, *Toy Story* represents a major advancement in the motion picture industry.

16. _____________________ claim

Yes, I am proud of my Hispanic heritage, and I want my children and grandchildren to speak Spanish. But if bilingual classes leave a child illiterate in two languages, something is wrong. Statistics and studies are routinely quoted to shore up claims that children learn better in their native language. That may be true for some children in bilingual programs, but that was not my experience. David and other Hispanic children are victims of a badly administered system more concerned with self-perpetuation than with students.

Ada Jimenez, "Trapped in the Bilingual Classroom"

INSTRUCTIONS: Match each type of type of claim, appeal, and assumption on the left with its definition on the right by writing the appropriate choice in each blank:

Logical Appeals

_______ 17. Fact

_______ 18. Statistic

_______ 19. Observation

_______ 20. Example

_______ 21. Analogy

Ethical Appeals

_______ 22. Author's Qualifications

_______ 23. Expert Opinion

Emotional Appeals

_______ 24. Appeal to Needs

_______ 25. Appeal to Values

A. A fact in the form of a number

B. A comparison meant to clarify or explain

C. Information about the author provided to increase the reader's confidence in the author's points

D. An attempt to identify the argument with readers' desires or needs

E. A specific case used to illustrate a general idea

F. An objectively verifiable type of evidence

G. An attempt to show that the author's conclusions are supported by other respected authorities

H. Evidence based on personal experience

I. An attempt to identify the argument with what readers think is important

---

INSTRUCTIONS: For each passage that follows, first identify the type of claim or thesis. Then identify the primary type of support used in each part of the passage indicated. Write the type of claim or support in the space above each selection:

Types of Claims	Types of Support	
Factual	Facts	Author's Qualifications
Value	Statistics	Expert Opinion
	Observations	Appeal to Needs
	Examples	Appeal to Values
	Analogy	

Passage 1

David G. Myers and Ed Diener, "The Pursuit of Happiness"

26.   Type of **claim** (thesis): _______________________

People are happier than one might expect, and happiness does not appear to depend significantly on external circumstances.

27.   Type of support: _______________________

We have found that the even distribution of happiness cuts across almost all demographic classifications of age, economic class, race and educational level. In addition, almost all strategies for assessing subjective well-being—including those that sample people's experience by polling them at random times with beepers—turn up similar findings.

28.   Type of support: _______________________

Alex Michalos of the University of Northern British Columbia and Ronald Inglehart of the University of Michigan, summarizing newer surveys of 18,000 university students in 39 countries and 170,000 adults in 16 countries, corroborate these findings.

29.   Type of support: _______________________

In study after study, four traits characterize happy people. First, especially in individualistic Western cultures, they like themselves. They have high self-esteem and usually believe themselves to be more ethical, more intelligent, less prejudiced, better able to get along with others, and healthier than the average person. . . . Second, happy people typically feel personal control. Those with little or no control over their lives—such as prisoners, nursing home patients, severely impoverished groups or individuals, and citizens of totalitarian regimes—suffer lower morale and worse health. Third, happy people are usually optimistic. Fourth, most happy people are extroverted. Although one might expect that introverts would live more happily in the serenity of their less stressed, contemplative lives, extroverts are happier—whether alone or with others.

30.   Type of support: _______________________

During the 1970s and 1980s, 39 percent of married adults told the National Opinion Research Center they were "very happy," as compared with 24 percent of those who had never married. In other surveys, only 12 percent of those who had divorced perceived themselves to be "very happy."

Passage 2

William J. Brennan Jr., "What the Constitution Requires"

31.   Type of support: _______________________

In 1956, Dwight D. Eisenhower appointed me to the Supreme Court. Now, at 90, I am frequently asked to identify the Court's greatest achievements in my 34-year tenure. High on my list is the protection of individual rights, dignity and self-determination.

32.   Type of support: _______________________

But we do not yet have justice for all who do not partake in the abundance of American life. One area of law more than any other besmirches the constitutional vision of human dignity. My old friend Justice Harry Blackmun called it the "machinery of death." It is the death penalty.

33.   Type of **claim** (thesis) : _______________________

The barbaric death penalty violates our Constitution.

34.   Type of support: _______________________

Even the most vile murderer does not release the state from its obligation to respect dignity, for the state does not honor the victim by emulating his murderer. Capital punishment's fatal flaw is that it treats people as objects to be toyed with and discarded.

35.   Type of support: _______________________

The task of nurturing the constitutional ideal of dignity does not rest solely with the nine Justices, or even with the cadre of Federal and state judges. We all share the burden.

INSTRUCTIONS: The following questions about assumptions refer to excerpts from Passage 1 above:

______   36.   By mentioning that "Alex Michalos of the University of Northern British Columbia and Ronald Inglehart of the University of Michigan . . . corroborate these findings," the authors are assuming that this will be acceptable support because

    A. their findings sound conclusive and very impressive.
    B. everyone knows approximately where these universities are.
    C. readers are likely have respect for university researchers.
    D. these researcher are Nobel prize winners.

_______ 37. The authors state that "In study after study, four traits characterize happy people" and then briefly explain what these traits are. They do this as support for their argument that "People are happier than one might expect, and happiness does not appear to depend significantly on external circumstances." What assumption are they making by offering these findings as support?

    A. Readers will recognize these traits as not dependent on external factors.
    B. Many readers will be able to identify with these characteristics.
    C. Most readers want to think of themselves as happy people.
    D. The studies referred to are well known to most readers.

INSTRUCTIONS: The following questions about assumptions refer to excerpts from Passage 2 above:

_______ 38. By beginning his article with the statements that "Dwight D. Eisenhower appointed me to the Supreme Court" and that he is "frequently asked to identify the Court's greatest achievements in my 34-year tenure" Justice Brennan assumes that readers will be impressed by his

    A. acquaintance with President Eisnhower.
    B. age.
    C. use of language.
    D. credentials.

_______ 39. The assumption Justice Brennan is making when he mentions his "old friend Justice Harry Blackmun" who referred to the death penalty as a "machinery of death" is that readers will

    A. agree with Blackmun's opinion of capital punishment.
    B. recognize the authority of a Supreme Court Justice and respect his view.
    C. be impressed by his friendship with a Supreme Court Justice.
    D. accept the fact the death penalty is unconstitutional.

_______ 40. Justice Brennan states that "the constitutional ideal of dignity" is a burden that "We all share." An assumption he is making in this statement is that readers will agree that the Constitution

    A. should be obeyed by all citizens.
    B. should indeed protect individual dignity.
    C. assigns responsibilities that are difficult to perform.
    D. represents the ideal document.

Chapter 10 Review:
Evaluating Arguments

_______ 1. *Analyzing* an argument involves determining

    A. why it has been written.
    B. the quality of the writing.
    C. how it is constructed.
    D. how well it is constructed.

_______ 2. To analyze an argument, you should

    A. identify the thesis and the support and determine the assumptions underlying the support.
    B. determine the quality of the writing in terms of the eloquence with which the author expresses ideas.
    C. judge how well the author supports the thesis and how reasonable the assumptions are that underlie the support.
    D. decide how thoroughly the author has discussed the topic of the article or essay.

_______ 3. *Evaluating* an argument then involves determining

    A. why it has been written.
    B. the quality of the writing.
    C. how it is constructed.
    D. how well it is constructed.

_______ 4. When evaluating an argument, you want to consider its *soundness*, which refers specifically to how

    A. effectively the author has supported the thesis.
    B. well the author has covered the material.
    C. concisely the author has expressed the ideas.
    D. clearly the author has stated the thesis.

_______ 5. When evaluating an argument, the first thing you want to do is

    A. criticize it.
    B. outline it.
    C. read it twice.
    D. analyze it.

INSTRUCTIONS: Once you have identified the author's thesis, you then want to determine how well the evidence actually supports the thesis. Then you want to evaluate the assumptions. An effective way to do this is to ask certain questions concerning the support and assumptions. Identify which of the questions below can be helpful in evaluating the support or the assumptions by writing the letter of one of the following choices in the space next to each question:

A. A question that helps evaluate the support
B. A question that helps evaluate an assumption

_______   6.   "Is the support based on what most people believe is important?"

_______   7.   "Is the support based on some commonly accepted truth?"

_______   8.   "Is the support directly related to the thesis?"

_______   9.   "Is the support based on a source of information that is generally considered trustworthy?"

_______   10. "Is there enough support to justify the claim?"

INSTRUCTIONS: Read the following excerpt from an argument that appeared on an Op-Ed page of the *New York Times*. Then answer the questions that follow it requiring you to evaluate it:

President Clinton promotes the wiring of the nation's high schools. Elementary schools seek grants for hardware and software. Colleges invest in video teaching systems. Yet the value of these expensive gizmos to the classroom is unproved and rests on dubious assumptions. . . .

Computers promise short cuts to higher learning. Today's educational software comes shrinkwrapped in the magic mantra: "makes learning fun."

Equating learning with fun says that if you don't enjoy yourself, you're not learning. I disagree. Learning takes work. Discipline. Responsibility—you have to do your homework. Commitment, from both teacher and students. There's no short cut to a quality education. And the payoff isn't an adrenaline rush but a deep satisfaction arriving weeks, months, or years later.

Anyway, what good are these glitzy gadgets to a child who can't pay attention in class, won't read more than a paragraph and is unable to write analytically?

Still, isn't it great that the Internet brings the latest events into classrooms? Maybe. Perhaps some teachers lack information, but most have plenty, thank you. Rather, there is too little class time to cover what's available. A shortage of information simply isn't a problem. . . .

Sure, students can search the Web, gathering information for assignments. The result? Instead of synthesizing a report form library sources, they often take the short cut, copying what's on line. . . .

Promoters of the Internet tell us that the World Wide Web brings students closer together through instant communications. But the drab reality of spending hours at a keyboard is one of isolation. While reaching out to faraway strangers, we're distancing from classmates, teachers and family. Somehow, I feel it's more important to pen a thank-you note to a friend than to upload e-mail to someone across the ocean.

Clifford Stoll, "Invest in Humanware"

_______   11.   Which of the following sentences from the article expresses the author's thesis, the central point of his argument?

    A. "President Clinton promotes the wiring of the nation's high schools."
    B. "Yet the value of these expensive gizmos to the classroom is unproved and rests on dubious assumptions."
    C. "Computers promise short cuts to higher learning."
    D. "Somehow, I feel it's more important to pen a thank-you note to a friend than to upload e-mail to someone across the ocean."

_______   12.   The author's first supporting point concerns his response to the claim that computers

    A. represent the answer to education's problems.
    B. offer short cuts to learning.
    C. enhance learning by making it fun.
    D. allow students increase communication through the Internet.

_______   13.   The author argues in his first supporting point that

    A. having fun is less important than learning the value of hard work.
    B. computers are not as much fun as their advocates claim.
    C. an adrenaline rush is less beneficial than hard work.
    D. the glitzy nature of computers make them very distracting for students.

_______   14.   By asking the question, "what good are these glitzy gadgets to a child who can't pay attention in class, won't read more than a paragraph and is unable to write analytically?" the author is making the assumption that readers

    A. value paying attention, reading, and writing more than having fun.
    B. know that most children have difficulty paying attention in class.
    C. have children of their own.
    D. want to improve education.

_______   15.   The author' second supporting point concerns his response to the claim that access to the Internet will enhance learning by

    A. demonstrating teachers' command of subject matter.
    B. making it easier to copy articles for use in research reports.
    C. increasing students' access to information about themselves.
    D. exposing students to information and increasing communication.

_______ 16. In his second supporting point, the author argues which **two** things?

   A. Teachers have enough information to pass on to students as it is.
   B. Children are incapable of dealing with more information.
   C. Communication in writing is more meaningful than via e-mail.
   D. Students need to learn to communicate their ideas more effectively.

_______ 17. The author states that ". . . there is too little class time to cover what's
available" and ". . . it's more important to pen a thank-you note to a friend
than to upload e-mail to someone across the ocean." In these statements, the
author is assuming that readers

   A. can relate to having too little time for the most important things.
   B. think personal interaction is more important than impersonal contact.
   C. will agree that computers offer access to information beyond the
       classroom.
   D. want to improve the educational system in any way they can.

_______ 18. Do the author's two supporting points directly relate to the thesis?

   A. Yes.
   B. No.

_______ 19. Does it seem that the author's two supporting points are enough support to
justify the claim

   A. Yes—the author provides logical appeals and evidence.
   B. No—the author presents only appeals to values with no facts.
   C. Yes—the author presents adequate factual evidence.
   D. No—the author should have included more of his own opinions.

_______ 20. The assumptions underlying the author's supporting points are based on

   A. commonly accepted truths.
   B. sources of information that are generally considered reliable.
   C. what most people believe is important.
   D. insupportable assertions.

_______ 21. Overall, it seems that the author's argument

   A. presents enough factual evidence to make his case convincing.
   B. will probably convince those who advocate computers in the classroom.
   C. will probably not convince readers who have never used a computer.
   D. appeals to what many readers value but presents no factual evidence.

_______ 22. This argument would probably be most convincing for readers who are

     A. avid computer users.
     B. teachers.
     C. uncomfortable with computers.
     D. school administrators.

_______ 23. In the title of this article, the author shows a bias for education that emphasizes

     A. teachers.
     B. investments.
     C. technology.
     D. creativity.

3

Generic Exercises/Quizzes

The following generic exercise/quizzes are meant to be used with whatever readings an instructor wants to assign to go along with the specific chapters in *Handbook for Critical Reading*. Refer to section 1, "Teaching with *Handbook for Critical Reading*" for a list of suggested anthologies, textbooks, other collections of readings, and news magazines that could be used to accompany this textbook. What follows are sets of exercise/quizzes that correspond to each of the ten chapters in *Handbook for Critical Reading*.

NAME _______________________________________

Reading Textbooks

INSTRUCTIONS: Complete the following items about a college textbook for one of your classes:

1. Textbook Title: ____

    Author(s):____

    Publisher:_______________________________ Latest Copyright Date:________________

    ____

    Meaning of Word: ____

2. Indicate the page numbers in the textbook on which the following are located. If one of these sections not included in your textbook, leave the space blank:

    Preface: _______________   Glossary: _______________

    Table of Contents: _______________   Index: _______________

    Appendices: _______________

3. Look through your textbook to find examples of the following types of graphic illustrations. Next to each type, write a page number where it is located in your text and the title of the graphic. If you can't find one, leave it blank:

	Page Number	**Title of Graphic Illustration**
Map:	_______________	_______________________________________
Diagram:	_______________	_______________________________________
Flow Chart:	_______________	_______________________________________
Pie Graph:	_______________	_______________________________________
Line Graph:	_______________	_______________________________________
Bar Graph:	_______________	_______________________________________
Table:	_______________	_______________________________________

INSTRUCTIONS: Next, refer to one specific chapter in your textbook to complete the following items:

4. Chapter Title: ____

    Chapter Page Numbers: _____________________________

5. Indicate the page numbers in the chapter on which the following are located. If one of these features is not included in your textbook, leave the space blank:

    Introduction: _______________   Chapter Summary: _______________

    List of Key Terms: _______________   Suggested Readings: _______________

    Review Questions: _______________

6. Now check the following features that your chapter includes:

    Marginal Notes: _________   Inserts: _________   Illustrations: _________

7. Take a few minutes to preview the chapter by skimming through and reading the introductory and concluding material and any other parts that could give you a general overview of the contents. Then briefly express in your own words what your previewing suggests that the chapter will focus on:

    ____

    ____

    ____

    ____

8. Write a multiple-choice question about something from the chapter, and circle the correct answer:

    ____

    ____

        a. ____

        b. ____

        c. ____

        d. ____

Harcourt Brace & Company

9.   Write an essay question that requires a broad understanding of the material discussed in the chapter. Then on a separate piece of paper, write what you feel is an acceptable answer for your question:

____

____

____

10. On separate paper, or in the space below, create an outline or a concept map that includes the main points discussed in the chapter. Then write a brief summary of the chapter that includes all the points listed on your outline or portrayed on your concept map.

NAME ____

Defining Words

Context Clues

INSTRUCTIONS: Look through a magazine, newspaper, or book, and find one sentence
for each of the following types of context clues. First, indicate the
publication in which you found each sentence. Then indicate the page
number on which you found the sentence, and write each sentence in
the appropriate space. Finally, circle the word that is defined by the
context of the sentence, and write the meaning of the word in the
space below:

Source: Title of Publication: ____

            Publication Date: _____________________________

1. **Definition Clue**: From page # ____________

    ____

    ____

    ____

    Meaning of Word: ____

2. **Explanation Clue**: From page # _________

    ____

    ____

    ____

    Meaning of Word: ____

3. **Synonym Clue**: From page # ____________

    ____

    ____

    ____

    Meaning of Word: ____

4.   **Restatement Clue:**   From page # _____________

____

____

____

Meaning of Word: ____

5.   **Antonym Clue:**   From page # _______________

____

____

____

Meaning of Word: ____

6.   **Example Clue:**   From page # _______________

____

____

____

Meaning of Word: ____

7.   **Surrounding Details Clue:**   From page # _____________

____

____

____

Meaning of Word: ____

8.   **Mood Clue:**   From page # _____________

____

____

____

Meaning of Word: ____

Word Parts

INSTRUCTIONS: Look through a magazine, newspaper, or book, and find one example of a word containing each of the following types of word parts. First, indicate the publication in which you found each word. Then indicate the page number on which you found the word, and write each word in the appropriate space. Finally, circle the word part, and write the meaning of the word in the space below:

Source: Title of Publication: ____

             Publication Date: _______________________________

Roots

1. _______________________________   From page # _______

     Meaning of Word: ___________________________________

2. _______________________________   From page # _______

     Meaning of Word: ___________________________________

3. _______________________________   From page # _______

     Meaning of Word: ___________________________________

4. _______________________________   From page # _______

     Meaning of Word: ___________________________________

Prefix Indicating an Amount or Proportion

5. _______________________________   From page # _______

     Meaning of Word: ___________________________________

Prefix Indicating Negative Meanings

6. _______________________________   From page # _______

     Meaning of Word: ___________________________________

Prefix Indicating a Direction or Relationship

7. _______________________________   From page # _______

  Meaning of Word: _______________________________

Prefix Indicating Time

8. _______________________________   From page # _______

  Meaning of Word: _______________________________

Suffix Forming an Adjective

9. _______________________________   From page # _______

  Meaning of Word: _______________________________

Suffix Forming an Adverb

10. _______________________________   From page # _______

  Meaning of Word: _______________________________

Suffix Forming a Noun

11. _______________________________   From page # _______

  Meaning of Word: _______________________________

Suffix Forming a Verb

12. _______________________________   From page # _______

  Meaning of Word: _______________________________

Harcourt Brace & Company

Dictionary Entries

INSTRUCTIONS: In a dictionary, locate one entry that contains all of the following features. Indicate the dictionary you have used and the page number on which you found the entry. Then write each of the parts of the entry into the appropriate spaces provided below. When you indicate the part of speech and word origin, write out the complete words rather than using the abbreviations that are in the entry:

Source: Title of Dictionary: ____

Publication Date: ____________   Entry from Page # _________

Main Entry: ________________________________

Pronunciation: ____

Part of Speech: ________________________________

Definitions: ____

____

____

Synonyms: ____

Related Forms: ____

Label: ________________________________

Word Origin: ____

Harcourt Brace & Company

Recognizing Main Ideas

INSTRUCTIONS: Read an article from a magazine or newspaper or a passage from a book that is at least two pages long. Then write your responses to the following items:

1.   Express the topic of the article in your own words:

   ____

2.   Briefly explain how you determined that this is the topic of the article:

   ____

   ____

3.   Is there a sentence or sentences that state the thesis or main ideas of the article? If so, explain where this is located in the passage:

   ____

4.   Paraphrase the sentence or sentences that state the main idea of the article:

   ____

   ____

   ____

5.   Briefly explain how you determined that this is the main idea of the article:

   ____

   ____

   ____

6. Now list, in a few words for each, the main supporting details from each paragraph or set of related paragraphs from the article, and number them in the order in which they appear. Use your own words as much as you can to paraphrase these supporting points:

Identifying Organizational Patterns

Transitions

INSTRUCTIONS: Look through a magazine, newspaper, or book, and find one sentence or pair of sentences for each of the types of transitions listed below. Indicate the publication in which you found each sentence. Then indicate the page number on which you found the sentence, and write each sentence in the appropriate space. Finally, circle the transitional word or phrase in the sentence:

Source: Title of Publication: ____________________________________

Publication Date: ____________________________

1. Addition: From page # __________

____

____

2. Time order: From page # __________

____

____

3. Location: From page # __________

____

____

4. Definition: From page # __________

____

____

5. Clarification: From page # __________

____

____

6. Emphasis: From page # _________

____

____

7. Classification: From page # _________

____

____

8. Comparison: From page # _________

____

____

9. Contrast: From page # _________

____

____

10. Cause and effect: From page # _________

____

____

11. Illustration: From page # _________

____

____

12. Summary: From page # _________

____

____

Organizational Patterns

INSTRUCTIONS: Read a magazine or newspaper article or a passage from a book, and try
to identify paragraphs or sets of paragraphs that exemplify the patterns
of organization listed below. First, indicate the information about the
article you have chosen. Then number the paragraphs in the article
and indicate in the appropriate spaces below which paragraph number
represents which pattern. Use more than one page if you need to use
more than one article to find examples of all of these organizational
patterns:

Source: Title of Publication: ______________________________________

____

Title of Article: ____

Author(s) of Article: _____________________________________

Publication Date: _______________   Page Numbers of Article: _____________

Paragraph #   **Pattern of Organization**

____________   Enumeration

____________   Classification

____________   Chronological Order

____________   Process

____________   Spatial Order

____________   Definition and Example

____________   Clarification through Example

____________   Comparison/Contrast

____________   Analogy

____________   Cause and Effect

____________   Problem/Solution

NAME _______________________________________

Using Inference

Making Inferences and Drawing Conclusions

INSTRUCTIONS: Read a magazine or newspaper article or a passage from a book, and find statements in which the author implies something without coming right out and saying it. Then copy five of these statements in the appropriate spaces below; under each one, explain the inference you can draw from the statement. Also, indicate below the publication that you have used, including the page number on which you found the statement you used:

Source: Title of Publication: _______________________________________

Title of Article: _______________________________________

Author(s) of Article: _______________________________________

Publication Date: ____________   Page Numbers of Article: ____________

1. Statement that implies something: From page # ________

____

____

____

The inference you can make from this statement:

____

____

2. Statement that implies something: From page # ________

____

____

____

The inference you can make from this statement:

____

____

3.   Statement that implies something: From page # _______

____

____

____

____

The inference you can make from this statement:

____

____

4.   Statement that implies something: From page # _______

____

____

____

____

The inference you can make from this statement:

____

____

5.   Statement that implies something: From page # _______

____

____

____

____

The inference you can make from this statement:

____

____

Author's Purpose

INSTRUCTIONS: Look through a magazine, newspaper, or book, and find one article or passage that represents each of the author's purposes listed below. Then find one statement from each article that makes the author's purpose clear, and copy that statement in the appropriate space below. Also, indicate the publication you used, and then indicate the specific article used for each one, including the page number on which you found the statement:

Source: Title of Publication: _______________________________________

Publication Date: ____________________________

To Entertain:

Title of Article: _______________________________________

Author(s) of Article: _______________________________________

Page Numbers of Article: _____________   Statement From page # _________

____

____

____

____

To Inform:

Title of Article: _______________________________________

Author(s) of Article: _______________________________________

Page Numbers of Article: _____________   Statement From page # _________

____

____

____

____

To Persuade:

Title of Article: ____

Author(s) of Article: ____

Page Numbers of Article: ______________ Statement From page # __________

____

____

____

____

____

Author's Tone

INSTRUCTIONS: Now look through a magazine, newspaper, or book, and find statements that represent the three tones listed below; then find three more statements that represent different tones. Copy each statement in the appropriate spaces below. For the three tones that you will name, indicate the tone of the statement in the appropriate blank. Also, indicate the publication you used and the page number on which you found each statement:

Source: Title of Publication: ____

Publication Date: ______________________________

Tone: __**Critical**__   From page # _______

____

____

____

Tone: <u>Objective</u>   From page # ______

____

____

____

Tone: <u>Respectful</u>   From page # ______

____

____

____

Tone: ______________________________   From page # ______

____

____

____

Tone: ______________________________   From page # ______

____

____

____

Tone: ______________________________   From page # ______

____

____

____

NAME ________________________________

Interpreting Language

INSTRUCTIONS: Look through a magazine, newspaper, or book, and find sentences using words with positive and negative connotations. Copy six of these sentences in the spaces below—three containing words with positive connotations and three containing words with negative connotations. Then circle the word in each sentence that has the positive or negative connotation. Also, indicate below the publication that you have used, including the page number on which you found each sentence:

Source: Title of Publication: ____

         Publication Date: ____________________

1. Sentence containing a word with a **positive** connotation: From page # ________

____

____

2. Sentence containing a word with a **positive** connotation: From page # ________

____

____

3. Sentence containing a word with a **positive** connotation: From page # ________

____

____

4. Sentence containing a word with a **negative** connotation: From page # ________

____

____

5. Sentence containing a word with a **negative** connotation: From page # ________

____

____

6. Sentence containing a word with a **negative** connotation: From page # _______

____

____

INSTRUCTIONS: Look through a magazine, newspaper, or book, and find sentences using euphemisms and idioms. Copy four of these sentences in the spaces below—two containing a euphemism and two containing an idiom. Then circle the word or phrase in each sentence that is either a euphemism or an idiom; and in the space provided, briefly explain its meaning. Also, indicate below the publication that you have used, including the page number on which you found each sentence:

Source: Title of Publication: ____

    Publication Date: _______________________

7. Sentence containing a **euphemism:**   From page # _______

____

____

Meaning:

____

8. Sentence containing a **euphemism:**   From page # _______

____

____

Meaning:

____

9. Sentence containing an **idiom:**   From page # _______

____

____

Meaning:

____

10.   Sentence containing an **idiom:**   From page # _________

____

____

Meaning:

____

INSTRUCTIONS: Look through a magazine, newspaper, or book, and find sentences containing the following types of figurative language. Copy one sentence for each in the appropriate space below; then in the next space, briefly explain its meaning. Also, indicate the publication that you have used, including the page number on which you found each sentence:

Source: Title of Publication: ____

          Publication Date: ____________________

11.   **Hyperbole:**   From page # _________

____

____

Meaning:

____

12.   **Irony:**   From page # _________

____

____

Meaning:

____

13. **Metaphor:**   From page # _________

____

____

Meaning:

____

14. **Simile:**   From page # _________

____

____

Meaning:

____

15. **Personification:**   From page # _________

____

____

Meaning:

____

16. **Symbolism:**   From page # _________

____

____

Meaning:

____

Reading Literature

INSTRUCTIONS: Define the following terms in your own words:

1. Literature:

   ____

   ____

2. Prose:

   ____

   ____

3. Poetry:

   ____

   ____

4. Nonfiction:

   ____

   ____

5. Fiction:

   ____

   ____

INSTRUCTIONS: Look through magazines, newspapers, or books, and find statements representing each of the following four modes of expression and two types of literary nonfiction. Copy one sentence in the appropriate space below that shows each mode or type of writing. Also, indicate the appropriate information about the articles and publications that you have used, including the page number on which you found each sentence:

1. Source: Title of Publication: ____

   Title of Article: ____

   Author(s) of Article: ____

   Publication Date: _______________   Page Numbers of Article: _______________

Description: From page # __________

____

____

____

2. Source: Title of Publication: ____

   Title of Article: ____

   Author(s) of Article: ____

   Publication Date: _______________   Page Numbers of Article: _______________

Narration: From page # __________

____

____

____

3. Source: Title of Publication: ____

   Title of Article: ____

   Author(s) of Article: ____

   Publication Date: _______________   Page Numbers of Article: _______________

Exposition: From page # __________

____

____

____

4. Source: Title of Publication: ____

              Title of Article: ____

              Author(s) of Article: ____

              Publication Date: _______________   Page Numbers of Article: ______________

Persuasion/Argumentation: From page # __________

____

____

____

5. Source: Title of Publication: ____

              Title of Article: ____

              Author(s) of Article: ____

              Publication Date: _______________   Page Numbers of Article: ______________

Essay: From page # __________

____

____

____

6. Source: Title of Publication: ____

              Title of Article: ____

              Author(s) of Article: ____

              Publication Date: _______________   Page Numbers of Article: ______________

Autobiography: From page # __________

____

____

____

Reading Fiction

INSTRUCTIONS: Read a short story from a magazine or book, and then write a few brief comments in the spaces below about each of the elements of fiction represented in the story. Also, indicate the appropriate information about the publication in which you have read the story:

Title of Publication: ____

Title of Short Story: ____

Author of Short Story: ____

Publication Date: ______________   Page Numbers of Story: ______________

Setting:

____

____

____

____

Characters:

____

____

____

____

Plot:

____

____

____

____

Point of View:

____

____

____

____

Theme:

____

____

____

____

Effect:

____

____

____

____

Reading Poetry

INSTRUCTIONS: Read a poem from a magazine or book, and then write a few brief comments in the spaces below about its arrangement and contents. First, describe the poem, suggesting how it reflects either a free verse arrangement or incorporates rhythm and rhyme. Then briefly comment on the contents in the appropriate spaces. Also, indicate the appropriate information about the publication in which you have read the poem:

Title of Publication: ____

Title of Poem: ____

Author of Poem: ____

Publication Date: _______________   Page Numbers of Poem: _______________

Arrangement (free verse, rhyme, rhythm):

____

____

____

Emotion:

____

____

____

____

Imagery:

____

____

____

____

Significance:

____

____

____

____

Effect:

____

____

____

____

Recognizing Persuasive Writing

Facts and Opinions

INSTRUCTIONS: Look through a magazine, newspaper, or book, and find sentences containing facts and opinions. Copy one sentence in each of the spaces below, according to whether it contains all facts, all opinion, or a combination of facts and opinions. For each sentence containing an opinion, circle any value words that reflect the opinion. Also, indicate the publication that you have used, including the page number on which you found each sentence:

Source: Title of Publication: ___________________________________

Publication Date: ___________________

Facts: From page # ________

____

____

Facts: From page # ________

____

____

Opinions: From page # ________

____

____

____

Opinions: From page # ________

____

____

____

Facts and Opinions: From page # ________

____

____

____

Facts and Opinions: From page # ________

____

____

____

Author's Bias

INSTRUCTIONS: Look through a magazine, newspaper, or book, and find a statement that represents an example of slanting and a statement that contains weasel words. Copy one statement in each of the spaces below, according to whether it shows slanting or contains weasel words. Then in the space following, briefly explain the bias that the statement is showing by the use of slanting or weasel words. Also, for each sentence containing a weasel word, circle the weasel word. Indicate the publication that you have used, including the page number on which you found each sentence:

Source: Title of Publication: ____

          Publication Date: _____________________

Slanting: From page # ________

____

____

____

Author's Bias:

____

Weasel Words: From page # _______

____

____

____

Author's Bias:

____

INSTRUCTIONS: Look through a magazine, newspaper, or book, and find statements that reflect an author's bias. Copy each statement in the spaces below; then in the space following, briefly explain what this statement suggests about what the author supports or opposes. Also, indicate the publication that you have used, including the page number on which you found each sentence:

Source: Title of Publication: _______________________________________

           Publication Date: _______________________

Biased Statement: From page # _______

____

____

____

Author's Bias:

____

Biased Statement: From page # _______

Author's Bias:

Recognizing Fallacies

INSTRUCTIONS: Look through a magazine, newspaper, or book, and find a sentence that represents an example of each of the types of fallacies indicated below. Copy one sentence in each of the spaces below. Also, indicate the publication that you have used, including the page number on which you found each sentence:

Source: Title of Publication: _______________________________________

               Publication Date: ___________________

Logical Fallacies with Irrelevant Support

Non Sequitur: From page # _______

Two Wrongs Make a Right: From page # _______

Red Herring: From page # _______

____

____

____

Logical Fallacies with Insufficient Support

Hasty Generalization: From page # _______

____

____

____

False Cause: From page # _______

____

____

____

False Comparison: From page # _______

____

____

____

False Dilemma: From page # _______

____

____

____

Harcourt Brace & Company

Appeal to Ignorance: From page # ________

____

____

____

Begging the Question: From page # ________

____

____

____

Circular Reasoning: From page # ________

____

____

____

Stacked Evidence: From page # ________

____

____

____

Ethical Fallacies

Argument to the Person: From page # ________

____

____

____

Straw Man: From page # ________

____

____

____

False Use of Authority: From page # _______

____

____

____

Emotional Fallacies

Appeal to the People: From page # _______

____

____

____

Appeal to Pity: From page # _______

____

____

____

Bandwagon Appeal: From page # _______

____

____

____

False Needs: From page # _______

____

____

____

Glittering Generalities: From page # _______

____

____

____

Slippery Slope: From page # _______

____

____

____

Analyzing Arguments

INSTRUCTIONS: Briefly answer the following questions:

1.   What is an argument?

   ____

2.   What is the purpose of the author's thesis in an argument?

   ____

3.   What is the purpose of the support in an argument?

   ____

4.   What is meant by the assumptions underlying the support?

   ____

INSTRUCTIONS: Look through a magazine, newspaper, or book, and find thesis statements from arguments that represent both factual and value claims. Copy each thesis statement in the appropriate spaces below. Also, indicate below the publication that you have used, including the page number on which you found each statement:

Source: Title of Publication: ________________________________

Publication Date: ________________

Factual Claim: From page # ________

____

____

Value Claim: From page # ________

____

____

Analyzing Arguments

INSTRUCTIONS: Read an argumentative essay in a magazine, newspaper, or a book that uses each of the types of logical support indicated below. Copy one sentence in the appropriate space for each type of support. Then briefly explain the assumption underlying this support that the author apparently feels will make it acceptable to readers. Also, indicate below the information about the article you have used, including a brief restatement in your own words of the author's thesis and the page number on which you found each type of support:

Logical Appeals

Title of Publication: ____

Title of Article: ____

Author(s) of Article: ____

Publication Date: _______________   Page Numbers of Article: ________

Type of Claim: ________________________

Thesis: ____

____

Types of Logical Support

Fact: From page # ________

____

____

____

Assumption:

____

Statistic: From page # ________

____

____

____

Assumption:

____

Observation: From page # _________

____

____

____

Assumption:

____

Example: From page # _________

____

____

____

Assumption:

____

Analogy: From page # _________

____

____

____

Assumption:

____

INSTRUCTIONS: Read an argumentative essay in a magazine, newspaper, or a book that uses each of the types of ethical support indicated below. Copy one sentence in the appropriate space for each type of support. Then briefly explain the assumption underlying this support that the author apparently feels will make it acceptable to readers. Also, indicate below the information about the article you have used, including a brief restatement in your own words of the author's thesis and the page number on which you found each type of support:

Ethical Appeals

Title of Publication: ____

Title of Article: ____

Author(s) of Article: ____

Publication Date: _________________   Page Numbers of Article: _________

Type of Claim: _______________________

Thesis: ____

____

Types of Ethical Support

Author's Qualifications: From page # _______

____

____

____

Assumption:

____

Expert Opinion: From page # _______

____

____

____

Assumption:

____

INSTRUCTIONS: Read an argumentative essay in a magazine, newspaper, or a book that uses each of the types of emotional support indicated below. Copy one sentence in the appropriate space for each type of support. Then briefly explain the assumption underlying this support that the author apparently feels will make it acceptable to readers. Also, indicate below the information about the article you have used, including a brief paraphrase of the author's thesis and the page number on which you found each type of support:

Emotional Appeals

Title of Publication: ____

Title of Article: ____

Author(s) of Article: ____

Publication Date: _________________   Page Numbers of Article: _______

Type of Claim: _____________________

Thesis: ____

____

Types of Emotional Support

Appeal to Needs: From page # _______

____

____

____

Assumption:

____

Appeal to Values: From page # _______

____

____

____

Assumption:

____

Evaluating Arguments

INSTRUCTIONS: Read an argument in a magazine, newspaper, or a book, and indicate below the information about the article you have read. Then respond to the items that follow concerning the thesis, support, assumptions, and your overall evaluation of the argument:

Title of Publication: ___________________________________

Title of Article: ___________________________________

Author(s) of Article: ___________________________________

Publication Date: ________________   Page Numbers of Article: _________

Thesis: Restate the author's thesis in your own words:

____

____

What type of claim is this?

____

Support and Assumptions: Paraphrase the main supporting points provided by the author. Also, indicate the type of support, and briefly explain the assumption underlying each support:

1.   Type of Support: ___________________________________

____

____

Assumption:

____

2.   Type of Support: ___________________________________

____

____

Assumption:

____

3. Type of Support: ______________________________

    ____

    ____

    Assumption:

    ____

4. Type of Support: ______________________________

    ____

    ____

    Assumption:

    ____

5. Type of Support: ______________________________

    ____

    ____

    Assumption:

    ____

6. Type of Support: ______________________________

    ____

    ____

    Assumption:

    ____

7. Type of Support: ______________________________

    ____

    ____

    Assumption:

    ____

After analyzing the argument, do you feel there is enough support to justify the claim?
Briefly explain why or why not:

____

____

____

Do you feel that the support is directly related to the thesis? Briefly explain:

____

____

____

Now, consider whether or not the author's assumptions make the support effective. Do you
feel that any of the support is based on some commonly accepted truth? Briefly explain:

____

____

____

Is any of the support based on sources of information that are generally considered reliable?
Briefly explain:

____

____

____

Is any of the support based on what most people commonly believe is important? Briefly
explain:

____

____

____

Now, write an evaluation of the argument you have read and just analyzed. Express how sound you feel the argument is by considering how well the support and assumptions relate to the thesis. In other words, discuss your answer to the question, "Do you think the argument is convincing?" Explain by referring to specific support and assumptions and to the thesis:

4

Exercises/Quizzes

for Specific Readings

All are included in Thomas Barnwell and Leah McCraney (Eds.),
An Introduction to Critical Reading, Third Edition
(Harcourt Brace, 1997)

Following the answer key, you will find duplicable handouts that can be used with the specific readings either as exercises to complete while reading the selection or as quizzes to be given afterwards. The title of each corresponds to a chapter in *Handbook for Critical Reading*, with each exercise/quiz focused on a specific reading skill or topic. The items in each one include questions regarding the contents of the reading selection indicated and require students to apply what they have learned from a chapter in *Handbook for Critical Reading*. All of the selections that these exercise/quizzes refer to can be found in the developmental reading textbook *An Introduction to Critical Reading*, Third Edition, by Thomas Barnwell and Leah McCraney(Harcourt Brace, 1997).

Exercise/Quiz for Specific Readings

Answer Key

Reading A Textbook Chapter: "Social Responsibility and Business Ethics" by Louis E. Boone and David Kurtz *Contemporary Business* (The Dryden Press, 1994, pages 96–131).

1. C

2. Businesses should act with a sense of social responsibility and out of ethical consideration.
   (or something similar)

3. surveying, questioning, marking, annotating, notetaking, reciting
   (or other reasonable responses)

4. B

5. A

6. D

7. C

8. B

9. A and D

10. Thesis: The importance of social responsibility and business ethics

A. Self-regulation
B. Government regulation
C. Evaluating social performance

A. Responsibilities to the public
B. Responsibilities to customers
C. Responsibilities to employees
D. Responsibilities to investors
 (or other reasonable responses)

Defining Words: "Introduction" by Karen Arms and Pamela S. Camp, from *Biology* (Saunders College Publishing, 1995, pages 1–13)

1. Individual animals, plants, fungi, algae, protozoa, and bacteria on earth.
 Definition.
 (Dictionary definitions will vary)

2. Still in the egg.
 Surrounding Details.
 (Dictionary definitions will vary)

3. Theory, a testable idea.
 Explanation, example.
 (Dictionary definitions will vary)

4. A group with no treatment.
 Antonym (experimental), example.
 (Dictionary definitions will vary)

5. Accepted beliefs.
 Explanation.
 (Dictionary definitions will vary)

6. Biologist: (literally) Someone who speaks about life; Someone who studies life

 bio: life, living

 log-: speech, discourse

 -ist: one who does, is, or believes in

7. Component: (literally) Performing together; parts working together

 com-: together, with

 -ent: causing, promoting, performing

8. Untestable: (literally) not able to be tested

 un-: not   test

 -able: able to be, capable of

9. Correlation: (literally) In a state of relating with

 co-: together, with   relate

 -ion: a state ,condition, action, or process

10. Depend: (literally) to hang down; to rely on

 de- away, down, from

 pend: hang

11. Extend: (literally) to stretch out or away from

 ex-: out, away from

 tend: stretch

12. Disadvantageous: (literally) not having the qualities of being toward a position; lacking an adequate position

 dis-: apart, away, not

 ad-: to, toward   vantage (position)

 -ous: full of, having the qualities of

Recognizing Main Ideas: "The Presidency in Crisis" by Joseph R. Conlin, from *The American Past: A Survey of American History* (Harcourt Brace College Publishers, 1993,   pages 806–823)

1. Crises during the Nixon, Ford, and Carter presidencies (or something similar)

2. B

3. A

4. A

5. E

6. B

7. D

8. A

9. C

10. B

11. C

12. D

13. C

14. B

15. Carter's greatest success was the peace agreement he helped forge between Israel and Egypt. (or something similar)

Identifying Organizational Patterns: "Mother Tongue" by Amy Tan

1. C

2. A

3. Circled "And" Addition

4. Circled "until" Time order

5. Circled "as well," "And, " "then," "because," "and" A

6. Time order or chronological During or Later

7. Contrast Yet or but

8. Contrast But

9. Cause and effect Because

10. Clarification through example One time

11. Time order or chronological five days ago, a month ago, Still, until, when,

12. Cause and effect effect, influenced by, because

13. Clarification through example such as, like

14. Cause and effect because, why

15. Time order or chronological after

Using Inference: "Confessions of a Female Chauvinist Sow" by Anne Richardson Roiphe and "Friendships Among Men" by Marc Feigen Fasteau

1. C
2. persuade or convince
3. A
4. A
5. C
6. B
7. B
8. persuade or convince
9. A
10. C
11. D
12. B
13. stereotypes

Interpreting Language: "Revelation" by Flannery O'Connor

1. negative
2. A
3. C
4. D
5. life, clothes, B
6. Many different types of people are needed for society to operate effectively. (or something similar).
7. D
8. B
9. B
10. God
11. metaphor, simile
12. Mrs. Turpin realizes that the social order she has believed in is not the same as the divine order. She sees that her behavior alone has not made her worthy of heaven. (or something similar)
13. religious, crazy, truth (or something similar)

Reading Literary Nonfiction: "A Hanging" by George Orwell

1. A
   C
2. 10
3. B
4. B
5. D
6. A
7. C
8. A
9. tragic
   playful (or something similar)
10. alive, with dignity (or something similar)
11. relieved (or something similar)
12. The author realized that it was wrong to kill another living human being, who still had all his faculties and still had his dignity. (or something similar)

Reading Short Fiction: "The Chrysanthemums" by John Steinbeck

1. A	6. C	11. B
2. A	7. B	12. D
3. C	8. D	13. A
4. C	9. D	14. B
5. D	10. B	

Reading Poetry: "I, Too" and "Harlem" by Langston Hughes

1. C	5. D	9. D
2. B	6. C	10. A
3. A	7. B	11. A
4. A	8. A	12. B

Recognizing Persuasive Writing: "Death and Justice" by Edward Koch and "The False Promise of Gun Control" by Daniel D. Polsby

1. The death penalty affirms life. (or something similar)
2. D
3. C
4. B
5. D
6. Gun control laws cannot solve the nation's crime problems. (or something similar)
7. B
8. fact, opinion
9. A
10. B
11. C

Analyzing Arguments: "Seven Doomsday Myths about the Environment" by Ronald Bailey and "A Planet in Jeopardy" by Lester R. Brown, Christopher Flavin, and Sandra Postel

1. 2

2. There is no real evidence that we are facing a worldwide environmental disaster in the near future.
   (or something similar)

3. A

4. D

5. C

6. A, A

7. B

8. 7, 31, and 32

9. The world is now faced with such serious population and ecological problems that unless something is done soon, serious consequences will follow.
   (or something similar)

10. A

11. D

12. C

13. B

14. Facts, believable or acceptable
    (or something similar)

15. B

Evaluating Arguments: "Does America Still Exist" by Richard Rodriguez

1. C

2. A

3. D

4. D

5. C

6. B

7. Resistance to assimilation is itself a characteristic of American culture.
   (or something similar)

8. C

9. A

10. separate groups, united by a common culture
    (or something similar)

11. B

12. his own opinions and personal experience
    (or something similar)

13. qualified to comment on American culture from an immigrant's perspective.
    (or something similar)

14. Responses will vary, but accept any that seem reasonable and that comment on the relevance and sufficiency of the support.

Reading A Textbook Chapter:
"Social Responsibility and Business Ethics"
by Louis E. Boone and David Kurtz,
from *Contemporary Business* (The Dryden Press, 1994)

_______ 1. From the list of "Learning Goals" on the first page of the chapter, it seems that the authors want readers to come away from this chapter with an understanding of

    a. social ethics.
    b. business operations.
    c. business responsibilities.
    d. responsibilities to customers.

2. From surveying the chapter, it seems that the main point the authors are making about the topic is that

____

____

____

3. List some of the most effective strategies to use if your purpose for reading this chapter is to learn the information for a test in a course:

_______________________________   _______________________________

_______________________________   _______________________________

_______________________________   _______________________________

_______ 4. Figure 4.1 portrays a business organization in a

    a. table.
    b. flow chart.
    c. diagram.
    d. line graph.

_______ 5. The margin notes that appear throughout the chapter are used to

    a. define important terms.
    b. summarize main points.
    c. highlight interesting ideas.
    d. outline the main ideas.

______ 6. In a few places in the chapter, there are what the authors call "Business Challenges" presented in boxes set off from the main text. These are

    a. marginal notes that summarize important ideas.
    b. reviews of some key points made up to that point in the text.
    c. lists of important terms and concepts discussed so far.
    d. inserts that provide interesting additional information.

______ 7. Figure 4.3 is a bar graph showing that in general

    a. men and women earn about the same.
    b. women earn more than men.
    c. men earn more than women.
    d. men and women both earn less now than in the past.

______ 8. The "Summary of Learning Goals" near the end of the chapter
    a. raises provocative issues that responsible businesses must address.
    b. sums up the main points made about each of these in the chapter.
    c. lists key concepts that readers should understand.
    d. provides thoughtful comments for readers to ponder.

______ 9. The "Key Terms," "Review Questions," and "Discussion Questions" at the end of the chapter can be useful for

    a. reinforcing what has been learned.
    b. outlining the chapter.
______   c. gaining an overview of the contents.
    d. studying for a test.

10. List the broadest main points made in the chapter to complete the following framework for an outline of the chapter:

Thesis: ____

    I. Being socially responsible

        A. ____________________________

        B. ____________________________

        C. ____________________________

    II. Types of Social Responsibilities

        A. ____________________________

        B. ____________________________

        C. ____________________________

        D. ____________________________

NAME ___________________________________

Defining Words:
"Introduction" by Karen Arms and Pamela S. Camp,
from *Biology* (Saunders College Publishing, 1995)

INSTRUCTIONS: Define the following words from the chapter. First, define each word according to its context, and indicate the type of context clue that helped you figure out its meaning. Then, using a dictionary, look up its meaning and write in the definition that matches how the word is used in the text:

1.   **Organisms** (first page, left column, second paragraph)

   Definition Suggested by the Context: _______________________________________

   ____

   Type of Context Clue: _______________________________

   Dictionary Definition: ____

2.   **Embryonic** (fourth page, right column, second paragraph)

   Definition Suggested by the Context: _______________________________________

   ____

   Type of Context Clue: _______________________________

   Dictionary Definition: ____

3.   **Hypothesis** (seventh page, right column, last paragraph)

   Definition Suggested by the Context: _______________________________________

   ____

   Type of Context Clue: _______________________________

   Dictionary Definition: ____

●   Harcourt Brace & Company

4. **Control** (eighth page, left column, first paragraph)

   Definition Suggested by the Context: ___________________________________

   ____

   Type of Context Clue: _______________________________

   Dictionary Definition: _______________________________________

5. **Dogmas** (eleventh page, left column, third paragraph)

   Definition Suggested by the Context: ___________________________________

   ____

   Type of Context Clue: _______________________________

   Dictionary Definition: _______________________________________

INSTRUCTIONS: Define the following words from the chapter according to the meaning of their word parts. Write in the meaning of the word parts composing the word, and write in a definition of the word that these word parts suggest:

6. **Biologist** ____

   bio _________________   **log-** ___________________________

   -ist ___________________________

7. **Component** ____

   com- _______________   **-ent** ___________________________

8. **Untestable** ____

   un- _______________   test   **-able** ___________________________

9. **Correlation** ____

   co- _______________   relate   **-ion** ___________________________

10. **Depend** ____

    de- ________________   **pend** ________________________

11. **Extend** ____

    ex- ________________   **tend** ________________________

12. **Disadvantageous** ________________________________

    dis- ________________   **ad-** ____________________________

    vantage (position)   **-ous** ________________________________

NAME ________________________________

1. Express in your own words a brief phrase that states the general topic of this textbook chapter:

    ____

______ 2. The first part of the chapter—"The Nixon Presidency"—focuses on

    A. foreign affairs.
    B. domestic affairs.
    C. economic issues.
    D. election campaigns.

______ 3. The best statement of the main idea for the section headed "Reshaping the Supreme Court" is that Nixon

    A. moved quickly to reshape the Supreme Court.
    B. chose Warren Burger of Minnesota to replace the retiring Chief Justice Earl Warren.
    C. made a serious error by insisting that the South have a Supreme Court justice.
    D. formed a Supreme Court that made no fundamental changes in the Warren Court rulings.

______ 4. Which of the following is the topic sentence in the first paragraph of the second part of the chapter, "Nixon's Vietnam"?

    A. "No foreign problem was so pressing as the ongoing war in Vietnam."
    B. "Nixon knew well that Lyndon Johnson's political career had been prematurely snuffed out by the agonizing, endless conflict."
    C. "Nixon wanted out of the war."
    D. "But how to turn the trick?"

INSTRUCTIONS: Fill in the outline below for the section "Expanding the War." Provide the main idea and major supporting points in the appropriate order from choices on the right:

5. Main Idea: ______________   A. Criticism and protest

6.   A. ______________   B. Couldn't pull out of the war

7.   B. ______________   C. Congress reacts

8.   C. ______________   D. Increased bombing and attacks

9.   D. ______________   E. Nixon's expansion of the war

_______ 10. The main point made in the section "Nixon-Kissinger Foreign Policy" is that

   A. the Vietnam War was just a "sideshow" to Nixon and Kissinger.
   B. Nixon and Kissinger wanted to completely reorder relations among the great powers.
   C. foreign policy during the Nixon administration was as much Kissinger's as it was Nixon's.
   D. the centerpiece of Nixon's foreign policy was détente with the Soviet Union.

_______ 11. Kissinger's "shuttle diplomacy" took its name from his efforts to

   A. carry out Nixon's foreign policy as effectively as possible.
   B. end the war in Vietnam as quickly as possible.
   C. travel back and forth between Middle Eastern countries trying to work out a peace arrangement.
   D. ease Cold War tensions by shuttling from country to country whenever conflicts erupted that threatened détente.

_______ 12. The first half of the section "Watergate and Gerald Ford" focuses mainly on

   A. the election of 1972.
   B. Nixon's political agenda.
   C. the Ford administration.
   D. Nixon's fall from power.

_______ 13. In the section "A Ford, Not a Lincoln," the author portrays the Ford administration as

   A. bumbling and largely ineffective.
   B. distinguished mainly by Ford's pardoning of Nixon.
   C. undistinguished but a relief from Nixon's deception.
   D. neither supported by Congress nor the American people.

______ 14. In the introduction to the section "Quiet Crisis," the author suggests that Jimmy Carter was able to get elected president primarily because he

    A.   came out of nowhere.
    B.   was not associated with the federal government.
    C.   spoke with an appealing Southern accent.
    D.   was well liked by the media.

______ 15. Express in your own words, the main point the author makes about President Carter in the section "Peacemaking":

____

____

____

NAME ___________________________________

**Identifying Organizational Patterns:
"Mother Tongue" by Amy Tan**

_______ 1. Amy Tan's thesis in this essay is that her mother's use of language

    A. was less significant in her life than her personal integrity and intelligence.
    B. improved over the years until she finally mastered it.
    C. influenced how people perceived her and how the author grew up.
    D. was different at home than when she went out in public.

_______ 2. The overall pattern of organization of the essay is

    A. cause and effect.
    B. chronological order.
    C. clarification through example.
    D. analogy.

INSTRUCTIONS: For the following items, circle all the transitional words or phrases in each sentence or set of sentences that reflect relationships between ideas. Then write in the blank the type of relationships indicated:

3. "Language is a tool of my trade. And I use them all—all the Englishes I grew up with." (Paragraph 2)

    Type of relationship indicated by the transition: _______________________________

4. "The talk was going along well enough, until I remembered one major difference that made the whole talk sound wrong." (Paragraph 3)

    Type of relationship indicated by the transition: _______________________________

5. "My husband was with us as well, and he didn't notice any switch in my English. And then I realized why. It's because over the twenty years we've been together I've often used that same kind of English with him, and sometimes he even uses it with me." (Paragraph 4)

    Relationships indicated by the transitions: _______________________________,

_______________________________, and _______________________________._

Of these three relationships, the dominant or most important relationship between the ideas in the sentences above is

    _______ A. cause and effect.
    B. time order.
    C. comparison.
    D. addition.

Harcourt Brace & Company

INSTRUCTIONS: In the items that follow, write in what you feel is the main pattern of
organization of each of the paragraphs indicated. Then indicate a
transitional word or phrase from the paragraph that reflects that
pattern:

6.   **Paragraph 5**: Main Pattern of Organization: _______________________________________

A transition reflecting this pattern:_______________________________________

7.   **Paragraph 7**: Main Pattern of Organization: _______________________________________

A transition reflecting this pattern:_______________________________________

8.   **Paragraph 8**: Main Pattern of Organization: _______________________________________

A transition reflecting this pattern:_______________________________________

9.   **Paragraph 9**: Main Pattern of Organization: _______________________________________

A transition reflecting this pattern:_______________________________________

10.   **Paragraph 10**: Main Pattern of Organization: _______________________________________

A transition reflecting this pattern:_______________________________________

11.   **Paragraph 14**: Main Pattern of Organization: _______________________________________

A transition reflecting this pattern:_______________________________________

12.   **Paragraph 15**: Main Pattern of Organization: _______________________________________

A transition reflecting this pattern:_______________________________________

13.   **Paragraph 16**: Main Pattern of Organization: _______________________________________

A transition reflecting this pattern:_______________________________________

14.   **Paragraph 18**: Main Pattern of Organization: _______________________________________

A transition reflecting this pattern:_______________________________________

15.   **Paragraph 19**: Main Pattern of Organization: _______________________________________

A transition reflecting this pattern:_______________________________________

Using Inference:
"Confessions of a Female Chauvinist Sow" by Anne Richardson Roiphe and "Friendships Among Men" by Marc Feigen Fasteau

_______ 1. Which of the following statements best sums up Roiphe's main point?

A. The experience of women clearly shows men to be morally inferior.
B. Women are more people-oriented than men.
C. If women really want social equality, they must accept men as equals.
D. Women have the moral responsibility to work toward a nonsexist society.

2. Considering Roiphe's main point and the way in which she discusses the topic, it

seems that her purpose is primarily to ____.

_______ 3. In the first paragraph, Roiphe implies that her father

A. is not the type of man she would like for a husband.
B. was not really as wonderful a person as she thought when growing up.
C. represents her ideal of a good husband.
D. was very handsome but not so intelligent.

_______ 4. In the fourth paragraph, the author describes her experiences with boys as she was growing up. From her experiences as a girl, Roiphe seems to have drawn the conclusion that

A. males are inferior to females.
B. boys and girls will never understand one another.
C. men are less concerned with women than with themselves.
D. girls should always be distrustful of boys.

_______ 5. The tone of paragraph 13 is primarily

A. ironic.
B. indignant.
C. humorous.
D. objective.

_______ 6. However, in paragraph 14, Roiphe suggests that women should not

A. be so frivolous at card games.
B. be so prejudiced against men.
C. allow men to have such influence over them.
D. have abortions without the father's consent.

_____ 7. The main point made by Fasteau in his essay is that

    A. men tend to be functional, competitive, unemotional, and independent.
    B. the male stereotype leads men to less than satisfying relationships.
    C. men should reject socially approved ideals and values.
    D. men tend to be too competitive.

8. Considering Fasteau's main point and the way in which he discusses the topic, it seems that his purpose is primarily to _______________________________.

_____ 9. In the third paragraph, Fasteau implies that he

    A. gave little thought to friendships as he was growing up.
    B. had few real friends as a boy.
    C. learned the real meaning of friendship in college.
    D. was a loner until he got to college.

_____ 10. In paragraph 8, the author states that "There are exceptions, but they only prove the rule." By saying this, and through the examples that follow in paragraphs 9–11, Fasteau is suggesting that the stereotype of men as untalkative is basically

    A. a myth.
    B. unsupported by evidence.
    C. true.
    D. a creation of women.

_____ 11. In paragraphs 23–26, the author discusses the effects of the fear of homosexuality on male relationships. The tone of Fasteau's comments suggests that what he describes

    A. disgusts him.
    B. scares him.
    C. angers him.
    D. saddens him.

_____ 12. In paragraph 27, Fasteau implies that men are uncomfortable

    A. in large group activities with other men.
    B. in individual relationships with other men.
    C. with women generally.
    D. with men outside their social circle.

13. Both Roiphe and Fasteau suggest that problems are caused for women and men because of social _______________________________.

Interpreting Language:
"Revelation" by Flannery O'Connor

______ 1. In the first paragraph, Mrs. Turpin is described as "looming at the head of the magazine table. . . ." The word "looming" has a ________________________ connotation.

______ 2. By describing a mother and child in paragraph 20 as "kind of vacant and white-trashy, as if they would sit there until Doomsday if nobody called and told them to get up," Mrs. Turpin seems to perceive them as

    A. poor and lacking initiative.
    B. smelly and lazy.
    C. poorly dressed and asleep.
    D. poor but religious-minded.

______ 3. Also in paragraph 24, Mrs. Turpin mentions people who had "good blood." This expression uses the word "blood" to mean

    A. parents.
    B. health.
    C. genes.
    D. red corpuscles.

______ 4. In paragraph 26, Mrs. Turpin refers to the clock in the doctor's waiting room as being "right on the dot." By this she means that it is

    A. small.
    B. pretty.
    C. similar to her watch.
    D. accurate.

5. In paragraph 53, Mrs. Turpin thinks to herself that a person should not just sit around the Courthouse when "you ain't got a thing but breath and britches." What she really means by "breath" is ________________ and by "britches" is ________________. And what she is actually saying is that a person should not just sit around if he or she is ______________.

    A. healthy
    B. poor
    C. unemployed
    D. free

6. What is meant by the common expression that Mrs. Turpin uses in paragraph 60, "it takes all kinds to make the world go around"?

______ 7. In paragraph 78, the ugly girl looks at Mrs. Turpin with "eyes fixed like two drills." This simile suggests that the girl was looking

    A. painfully.
    B. perceptively.
    C. quickly.
    D. intensely.

______ 8. After being rescued from the ugly girl, Mrs. Turpin in paragraph 103 feels "entirely hollow except for her heart which swung from side to side as if it were agitated in a great empty drum of flesh." Apparently, Mrs. Turpin

    A. feels emotionally shaken and physically numb.
    B. feels nothing except for the rapid beating of her heart.
    C. has lost consciousness.
    D. is being lifted off of the floor.

______ 9. The description of Mrs. Turpin in paragraph 171 uses figurative language to suggest that she feels

    A. like crying.
    B. angry and disturbed.
    C. unable to find words to express herself.
    D. confused and dismayed.

10. Who is Mrs. Turpin speaking to in paragraph 178? ______________________________

11. The last sentence in paragraph 179 uses figurative language to describe the sun. "The sun was behind the wood, very red" is a ______________________, and "looking over the paling of the trees like a farmer inspecting his own hogs" is a

______________________.

12. In paragraph 191, Mrs. Turpin realizes something about what has happened to her that she seems to see in the sky. Briefly explain what she realizes:

____

____

____

13. The ugly girl's name, Mary Grace, is symbolic because both words in her name have ______________________ significance. The name is also ironic because she acted so ______________________ but forced Mrs. Turpin to see the ______________________.

NAME _______________________________

Reading Literary Nonfiction:
"A Hanging" by George Orwell

_______ 1. Which two of the following best describe the type of writing represented by Orwell's "A Hanging"?

   a. Narrative
   b. Exposition
_______ c. Autobiography
   d. Biography

_______ 2. In which paragraph does Orwell reflect on the meaning of what he has been describing?

_______ 3. Which sentence from the essay most clearly states Orwell's thesis?

   a. "But he stood quite unresisting, yielding his arms limply to the ropes, as though he hardly noticed what was happening." (paragraph 2)
   b. "When I saw the prisoner step aside to avoid the puddle I saw the mystery, the unspeakable wrongness, of cutting a life short when it is in full tide." (paragraph 10)
   c. "He and we were a party of men walking together, seeing, hearing, feeling, understanding the same world; and in two minutes, with a sudden snap, one of us would be gone—one mind less, one world less." (paragraph 10)
   d. "The dead man was a hundred miles away." (paragraph 24)

_______ 4. Orwell's purpose in this essay is to

   a. describe an execution that he witnessed.
   b. persuade readers that capital punishment is wrong.
   c. describe prison conditions in Burma at that time.
   d. entertain readers with a lively description.

_______ 5. Orwell describes the prisoner as a "puny wisp of a man" who is guarded by "six tall Indian warders." Details such as these are meant to

   a. alarm the reader.
   b. inform the reader.
   c. show the reader how dangerous the prisoner really was.
   d. show sympathy for the prisoner.

_______ 6. What we know for certain about the prisoner is that he was

   a. being executed.
   b. guilty of a crime.
   c. innocent of any crime.
   d. a murderer.

●

_______ 7. In paragraph 5, the superintendent's comments suggest that he is

    a. genuinely concerned about the prisoners in his care.
    b. a sadistic man.
    c. not very sympathetic toward the man to be hanged.
    d. an extremely efficient administrator.

_______ 8. On the way to the gallows, the prisoner and those accompanying him were interrupted by a dog that seemed to

    a. want to play with the prisoner.
    b. know that someone was going to die.
    c. deliberately try to prolong the prisoner's life.
    d. know the prisoner.

9. The episode with the dog is ironic because of the contrast between the situation which

is ___________________________________ and the dog's behavior which is _________

___________________________ .

10. When Orwell saw the prisoner step aside to avoid a puddle of water, he realized that

the prisoner was ____ .

11. After the hanging, Orwell and the others felt _______________________________ .

12. Summarize paragraph 10 by briefly expressing in your own words what Orwell says that he realized:

____

____

____

____

____

____

____

NAME _______________________________

Reading Short Fiction:
"The Chrysanthemums" by John Steinbeck

_______   1. The setting for this story is

    a. a ranch in the Salinas Valley in December.
    b. an unknown location.
    c. in California during the Spring.
    d. near a river on the Great Plains.

_______   2. The protagonist in the story is

    a. Elisa Allen.
    b. Henry Allen.
    c. the tinker.

_______   3. The antagonist in the story is

    a. Elisa Allen.
    b. Henry Allen.
    c. the tinker.

_______   4. The plot in the story involves

    a. a couple's struggle to define each other's roles.
    b. Elisa's attempt to escape an abusive situation.
    c. Elisa's desire for more in life than what she has.
    d. the tinker's attempt to influence Elisa's life.

_______   5. The narrator of this story is

    a. Elisa, looking back in time.
    b. someone who seems to knows the characters.
    c. an unknown friend of Elisa's
    d. omniscient.

_______   6. Which of the following statements most completely sums up the theme or central point of the story?

    a. Women are often limited to roles defined by men.
    b. People are often tempted by romantic strangers.
    c. The roots one has established are also limitations.
    d. Men are less sensitive and understanding than women.

_______   7. The overall effect of this story is to leave one with a sense of Elisa's

    a. regret.
    b. frustration.
    c. suspense.
    d. melancholy.

_______ 8. In the first paragraph, the setting is described as "closed off . . . from all the rest of the world" by a winter fog that surrounded the area "like a lid on the mountains and made of the great valley a closed pot." This description is symbolic of Elisa's situation in that her life is

   a. totally occupied by her chores on the ranch.
   b. determined by her own interests.
   c. limited to caring for her family.
   d. completely defined for her by her husband.

_______ 9. Elisa finds pleasure in

   a. raising her children.
   b. caring for her husband.
   c. reading.
   d. growing flowers.

_______ 10. Because of Henry's comments about her chrysanthemums in paragraphs 12–14, Elisa begins to wonder if

   a. her flowers are worth all the trouble.
   b. she can do more than she presently is.
   c. he is just trying to humor her.
   d. she could actually run the ranch.

_______ 11. The appearance of the tinker makes it clear that Elisa feels

   a. satisfied with her life as it is.
   b. dissatisfied with her life as it is.
   c. interested in learning new things.
   d. uninterested in learning new things.

_______ 12. Through most of paragraphs 71–106, Elisa feels

   a. aggressive and determined.
   b. shy but determined.
   c. fascinated but hesitant.
   d. strong and passionate.

_______ 13. Then after she sees that that tinker has thrown away the chrysanthemums, Elisa

   a. sadly accepts the impossibility of her life ever changing.
   b. realizes that a tinker's life is not what she had thought it might be.
   c. understands the value of the life she has with her husband.
   d. recognizes the dignity of a life of duty and roots.

_______ 14. The chrysanthemums in this story symbolize

   a. the wisdom that one gains from working in the earth.
   b. both the pleasure and pain that come from putting down roots.
   c. Elisa's desire to escape a frustrating existence.
   d. the duties and responsibilities of a woman's life on a ranch.

NAME ________________________________

Reading Poetry:
"I, Too" and "Harlem" by Langston Hughes

_______ 1. Throughout the poem "I, Too," Hughes uses the metaphors of the "kitchen" and the "table" to represent his desire to

    a. no longer have to cook.
    b. be allowed to eat with his employers.
    c. be accepted as an equal.
    d. be served a delicious meal.

_______ 2. When Hughes refers to "they" in line 3 of "I, Too," he is referring to

    a. Americans generally.
    b. the people he works for.
    c. white Americans.
    d. his sisters and brothers.

_______ 3. When Hughes in lines 5–7 of "I, Too" says he will "laugh," "eat well," and grow strong," he means that he will

    a. develop himself during his subservience.
    b. steal food from his employers.
    c. have as much fun in the kitchen as he can.
    d. deliberately ignore what he has been asked to do.

_______ 4. In "I, Too," Hughes says, "They'll see how beautiful I am/And be ashamed." By this he means that

    a. eventually white Americans will regret their discriminatory attitudes.
    b. one day white Americans will consider blacks to be their superiors.
    c. a revolutionary movement will transform American society.
    d. his employers will wish they had appreciated how attractive he actually is.

_______ 5. The tone in "I, Too" suggests that the author is expressing what attitude?

    a. Indigence
    b. Apathy
    c. Pessimism
    d. Optimism

_______ 6. In contrast to the poem "I, Too," the poem "Harlem" expresses an attitude that is much more

    a. indignant.
    b. apathetic.
    c. pessimistic.
    d. optimistic.

_______ 7. In "Harlem," Hughes uses metaphors to discuss the

   a. effects of a restless night of dreamless sleep.
   b. possible results of unrealized dreams.
   c. consequence of ignoring details.
   d. benefits of deferred gratification.

_______ 8. In "Harlem," Hughes begins by asking the question, "What happens to a dream deferred?" He answers this question by using metaphors to suggest that the ultimate result could be

   a. anger.
   b. disappointment.
   c. disillusionment.
   d. inspiration.

_______ 9. In "Harlem," which words used figuratively represent what Hughes suspects is the ultimate result of "a dream deferred"?

   a. "like a raisin in the sun"
   b. "like a sore"
   c. "like a syrupy sweet"
   d. "does it explode?"

_______ 10. In "Harlem," when Hughes says "Does it dry up like a raisin in the sun?", what he means is that

   a. a dream could become less important if it goes unrealized.
   b. one's goals are only attainable if they are realistic to begin with.
   c. there is a natural process that governs the fulfillment of a person's ambitions.
   d. modern society is as worthless as a withered grape.

_______ 11. In "Harlem," when Hughes says "Does it fester like a sore—/and then run?", he means that a having a dream can

   a. result in infection.
   b. be painful.
   c. be distracting.
   d. cause fatigue.

_______ 12. Considering what Hughes suggests in the poem "I, Too," the "dream deferred" in "Harlem" seems to refer to

   a. growth.
   b. equality.
   c. wealth.
   d. health.

Recognizing Persuasive Writing:
"Death and Justice" by Edward Koch and
"The False Promise of Gun Control" by Daniel D. Polsby

1. Edward Koch's thesis in "Death and Justice" is that

____

____

______ 2. Koch's uses in the first two paragraphs examples of convicted murderers apparently to represent those who condemn the death penalty. This is an example of

    A. figurative language.
    B. logical support.
    C. opinions masked as facts.
    D. slanting.

______ 3. In the sixth paragraph, Koch says, "If we create a society in which injustice is not tolerated, incidents of murder—the most flagrant form of injustice—will diminish." This is a statement of

    A. fact.
    B. fact and opinion.
    C. opinion.

______ 4. In paragraph 13, Koch states, "The execution of a lawfully condemned killer is no more an act of murder than is legal imprisonment an act of kidnapping." This statement is an example of

    A. fact.
    B. false comparison.
    C. two wrongs make a right.
    D. straw man.

______ 5. In paragraph 15, Koch states, "When we protect guilty lives, we give up innocent lives in exchange." This is an example of a false dilemma fallacy because it assumes that

    A. guilty lives should not be protected.
    B. the lives of innocent people are more important than the lives of the guilty.
    C. only the rights of the innocent should be considered.
    D. it is impossible to protect the rights of both the guilty and the innocent.

6.   Daniel Polsby's thesis in "The False Promise of Gun Control" is that

____

____

_______   7.   Judging by what Polsby says in paragraphs 2–3, he seems to feel that the passage of the Brady bill was

   A. necessary.
   B. a mistake.
   C. inevitable.
   D. a positive thing.

8.   In paragraph 3, the author states, "Current rates of crime and violence are a bit below the peaks of the late 1970s, but because of a slight oncoming bulge in the at-risk population of males aged fifteen to thirty-four, the crime rate will soon worsen." The first part of this statement is a(n) ______________________________, but the second part is a(n) ___________________.

_______   9.   In paragraph 35, Polsby states that "many journalists and a few public officials have already said, that we ought to treat guns the same way we do smallpox viruses or other critical vectors of morbidity and morality—namely, isolate them from potential hosts and destroy them as speedily as possible." A statement like this is an emotional fallacy because the author seems to misrepresent the views of the journalists and public officials referred to by suggesting that they support

   A. a ridiculous-sounding idea.
   B. total gun regulation.
   C. the control of infectious diseases.
   D. the deregulation of guns.

_______   10.   In paragraph 45, Polsby provides some statistics beginning with the sentence, "But as an educated guess . . ." and ending with "say, 100,000 executions in the next twenty years." These are examples of

   A. factual statements.
   B. opinions that appear to be facts.
   C. both facts and opinions.

_______   11.   Polsby's final statement in paragraph 57—"and honest folk must choose between being victims and defending themselves"— is an example of

   A. a factual statement.
   B. an appeal to ignorance.
   C. a false dilemma.
   D. an appeal to pity.

NAME ________________________________

Analyzing Arguments:
"Seven Doomsday Myths about the Environment" by Ronald Bailey and "A Planet in Jeopardy" by Lester R. Brown, Christopher Flavin, and Sandra Postel

1. Ronald Bailey's thesis in the article "Seven Doomsday Myths about the Environment" is first stated in paragraph # _________.

2. Restate Bailey's thesis in your own words:

____

____

_________ 3. What type of claim is this?

    A. Factual
    B. Value

_________ 4. Bailey attempts to support his thesis by

    A. providing compelling scientific findings.
    B. recounting his personal experiences.
    C. offering evidence of environmental problems.
    D. dispelling environmental doomsday myths.

_________ 5. Bailey's first supporting point is that

    A. because of dramatic population increases around the world, many areas will likely face widespread famines.
    B. the world's population has doubled since the end of World War II.
    C. global famine is not a threat primarily because increases in food production have outpaced population growth.
    D. agricultural technology has dramatically increased food crop yields.

6. This first supporting point is primarily a(n) _______ appeal, which provides ___________ as support.

    A. logical   A. facts and statistics
    B. ethical   B. expert opinion
    C. emotional   C. appeals to needs

_________ 7. When Bailey quotes Gale Johnson in paragraph 8, he is assuming that readers will

    A. trust the reliability of statistical data.
    B. feel confident in the opinion of a cultural economist from a major university.
    C. agree with what Johnson is quoted as predicting about the elimination of famine.
    D. see the agreement between what Johnson says and the quote from Paul Ehrlich in paragraph 5.

8.   In the article "A Planet in Jeopardy" by Lester R. Brown, Christopher Flavin, and Sandra Postel, the thesis is first stated in paragraph # _____________ and is then restated in paragraphs #__________ and #________________.

9.   Restate these authors' thesis in your own words:

____

____

_______   10.   What type of claim is this?

      A. Factual
      B. Value

_______   11.   Brown, Flavin, and Postel attempt to support their thesis mainly through

      A. personal observations, examples, and analogies.
      B. appeals to readers' needs and values.
      C. establishing their qualifications and quoting authorities.
      D. factual evidence and expert testimonies.

_______   12.   In paragraphs, 1–6, the authors quote Bruce Wallace's retelling of the story of the *Titanic* disaster. They do this in their introduction in the hope that readers will recognize this story as

      A. a frightening example of the dangers of international travel.
      B. factual evidence showing how pollution of the ocean can occur.
      C. an analogy that illustrates the situation faced by society now.
      D. an authority's personal observation in support of the thesis.

_______   13.   In paragraphs 21–25, the authors try to show the connection between environmental decline and

      A. life expectancy.
      B. increasing poverty.
      C. increasing population.
      D. economic output.

14.   The support provided in paragraphs 21–25 is mainly in the form of _________________, which the authors assume the readers will find to be _________________________________.

_______   15.   The authors end their argument in the final two paragraphs with an appeal to readers'

      A. logic.
      B. fear.
      C. common sense.
      D. sympathy.

NAME _______________________________

**Evaluating Arguments:
"Does America Still Exist" by Richard Rodriguez**

_______ 1.   Richard Rodriguez titles his essay with a question but provides no simple
answer. He begins in the first paragraph with the suggestion that

A. America exists as a distinct culture.
B. urban life exemplifies the variety of cultures in this country.
C. to immigrants, American cities seem to reflect a common culture.
D. the way of life in American cities represents a unique blend of cultures.

_______ 2.   In paragraphs 2–3, Rodriguez reflects on his own experience growing up as the
child of immigrant parents and suggests that he

A. felt like an American.
B. felt like a Mexican.
C. was encouraged by his parents to think of himself as a Mexican.
D. proudly proclaimed his American identitiy.

_______ 3. In paragraphs 4–5, Rodriguez suggests that immigrant groups have often felt

A. welcome in America.
B. confused about their identity.
C. enthusiastic about becoming Americans.
D. guilty about losing their traditional cultures.

_______ 4. In paragraph 6, the author states clearly that he feels

A. there is no identifiable American culture.
B. American culture is oppressive.
C. immigrants only hesitatingly assimilate.
D. there is definitely an American culture.

_______ 5. Then in paragraph 7, he states that Americans

A. wholeheartedly embrace a unifying culture.
B. long to return to the country of their ancestors.
C. try to cling to their individuality.
D. constantly attempt to recreate themselves.

_______ 6.   In paragraphs 8–9, Rodriguez contrasts America's rural Puritan heritage with
the more multicultural cities. Which does he feel most completely typify
American culture?

A. Rural areas.
B. the cities.

•

_______ 7. After a discussion of the Catholic and Indian cultures of Mexico, Rodriguez ends paragraph 12 by claiming that

____

_______ 8. In paragraphs 13–15, Rodriguez tries to show how schools

    A. alienate immigrant children.
    B. intimidate children.
    C. act as assimilating agents.
    D. teach children a patriotic attitude.

_______ 9. In paragraph 16, Rodriguez asks again the question from the title of the essay then goes on to discuss the Black civil rights movement (through paragraph 20), which he feels has

    A. resulted in feelings of ethnic separatism.
    B. contributed to a new national unity.
    C. led to harmonious relations between minority groups and the white majority.
    D. had profound effects on subsequent immigrant groups.

10. In paragraph 21–22, Rodriguez suggests what seems to be his thesis that Americans want to believe they are ____, but in reality they are _________________________________.

_______ 11. Rodriguez ends his essay mentioning the "little white girl rehearsing to herself a Motown obbligato," which he seems to feel represents

    A. an example of urban separateness.
    B. a metaphor for America's shared culture.
    C. the epitome of assimilation.
    D. all that is good about this country.

12. Throughout this essay Rodriguez relies for support almost entirely on

____.

13. By mentioning his own experience as a child of Mexican immigrants, Rodriguez probably assumes that readers will see him as

____.

14.   Considering Rodriguez's thesis and the support he offers, do you find his argument convincing? Briefly explain your evaluation in terms of whether the support is relevant and sufficient:

Acknowledgments

Unless otherwise indicated, everything in this instructor's manual has been written by Don Meagher. The following is a list of sources for previously copyrighted material quoted in the Review Exercises/Quizzes.

Agee, James. *Let Us Now Praise Famous Men.* (1960). Boston: Houghton Mifflin. (Quote from page 41)

Angier, Natialie. (April 30, 1996). "Illuminating How Our Bodies Are Built for Sociability," the *New York Times*, pages, B5, B8. (Quote from page B8)

Brennan, William J. Jr. (1996,). "What the Constitution Requires," the *New York Times*, April 28, page 13E.

Browning, Elizabeth Barrett, "XLIII," *Songs from the Portuguese*, Avenel Books. (Quote from page 102)

Buchwald, Art. (1984). *You Can Fool All of the People All the Time.* New York: Putnam's Sons. (Quote from page 326)

Coontz, Stephanie. (March 1995). "The American Family and the Nostalgia Trap," *Phi Delta Kappan*, pages K1–K20. (Quote from page K3)

Erdrich, Louise. *Love Medicine.* (1984). New York: Bantam Books. (Quote from page 216)

Frank, Anne. (1972). *The Diary of a Young Girl.* New York: Washington Square Press. (Quote from page 143)

Hallonen, Jane S., & John W. Santock (1996). *Psychology: Contexts of Behavior.* Madison: Brown & Benchmark Publishers. (Quote from page 706)

Hirsey, John. (1989). *Hiroshima.* New York: Vintage Books. (Quote from 16)

Jimenez, Ada. (February 3, 1996). "Trapped in the Bilingual Classroom," the *New York Times*.

Kolata, Gina. (April 21, 1996). "The Unwholesome Tale of the Herb Market," the *New York Times*, page 6E.

Le Batard, Dan. (December 29, 1994). "No! It's Joe: Sorry—The Rings Say It All." *The Miami Herald*, page 1D.

Lee, Harper. (1960). *To Kill a Mockingbird.* New York: Warner Books. (Quote from page 5)

Lohr, Steve. (April 21, 1996). "The Great Unplugged Masses Confront the Future," the *New York Times*, page E71, E6. (Quote from page E1)

Harcourt Brace & Company

Marks, Peter. (April 28, 1996). "Translations of the Bard: Perorations Devoutly to be Missed," the *New York Times*, page E7.

Mason, Jackie. (April 21, 1996). "Taking a P.C. to the Toilet," the *New York Times*, page E6.

Momaday, N. Scott. (1992). *In the Presence of the Sun*. New York: St. Martin's Press. (Quote from page 74)

Myers, David G., & Diener , Ed. (May 1996). "The Pursuit of Happiness," *Scientific American*, Pages 70–72. (Quote from page 70).

Raban, Jonathan. (May 20, 1996). "The Unlamented West," The *New Yorker*, pages 60–81. (Quote from page 60)

Rosin, Hanna. (May 13, 1996). "Working Girls," *The New Republic*, pages 11–12. (Quote from page 11).

Simon, Kate. (1982). *Bronx Primitive*. New York: Harper & Row. (Quote from pages 27–28)

Smith, Page. (1980). *The Shaping of America*. New York: McGraw-Hill. (Quote from pages 820–821)

Stoll, Clifford. (May 19, 1996). "Invest in Humanware," the *New York Times*, page 15E.

Stuckey-French, Elizabeth. (April, 1996). "Junior," the *Atlantic Monthly*, pages 90–102. (Quote from page 91)

Readings Referred to in the Exercises/Quizzes for Specific Readings
from
Thomas Barnwell and Leah McCraney (Eds.),
An Introduction to Critical Reading, Third Edition,
(Fort Worth: Harcourt Brace College Publishers, 1997).

Arms, Karen, and Pamela S. Camp. (1995). "Introduction," *Biology*. Philadelphia: Saunders College Publishing (pages 1–13).

Bailey, Ronald. (January-February 1995). "Seven Doomsday Myths about the Environment," *The Futurist*, pages 14–18.

Boone, Louis E., and Kurtz, David. (1994). "Social Responsibility and Business Ethics," *Contemporary Business*. Fort Worth: The Dryden Press (pages 96–131).

Brown, Lester R., Christopher Flavin, and Sandra Postel. (May–June 1992). "A Planet in Jeopardy," *The Futurist*, pages 10–14.

Conlin, Joseph R. (1993). "The Presidency in Crisis," *The American Past: A Survey of American History*. Fort Worth: Harcourt Brace College Publishers (pages 806–823).

Fasteau, Marc Feigen. "Friendships Among Men."

Hughes, Langston. (1959). "Harlem," and "I, Too," *Selected Poems of Langston Hughes*. Alfred A. Knopf.

Koch, Edward. (1981). "Death and Justice," *The New Republic*.

O'Connor, Flannery. "Revelation."

Orwell, George. (1978). "A Hanging," *Shooting an Elephant and Other Essays*. Harcourt Brace.

Polsby, Daniel D. "The False Promise of Gun Control."

Rodriguez, Richard. (1984). "Does America Still Exist," *Harper's Magazine*.

Roiphe, Anne Richardson. (1972). "Confessions of a Female Chauvinist Sow," *New York Magazine*.

Steinbeck, John. (1965). "The Chrysanthemums," *The Long Valley*. New York: Viking Penguin.

Tan, Amy. (1989). "Mother Tongue," *Threepenny Review*.